Parenting When Your Child is an Adult

Parenting When Your Child is an Adult

By **Dale M. Jacobs, MD**
and **Renee Gordon Jacobs, MSW**

ISBN 1-84333-629-4

A catalogue record for this book is available from the British Library

Published in 2003 by

Vega
Chrysalis Building
Bramley Road
London W10 6SP

An imprint of **Chrysalis** Books Group plc

Visit our website at www.chrysalisbooks.co.uk

Jacket design: Grade Design Consultants
Editor: Lisa Morris
Design: Roland Codd
Managing Editor: Laurence Henderson
Production: Susan Sutterby

Printed in Great Britain
by Creative Print and Design Wales, Ebbw Vale

We're threads on this loom

Woven together

Criss/Cross

Repeating patterns

Haiku by Paula Dyer

We dedicate this book
To our parents
Martha and Leroy Gordon
Harry and Helen Jacobs
And to all parents
Who try their best
In this uniquely challenging
and rewarding adventure

Acknowledgements

We could not have written this book without the tremendous help of our children, Rebecca, Joshua and Sarah. In our experience of raising them, we have learned so much together. While they are three terrific young adults, their lives have not always gone smoothly and we have not always responded in the most helpful way. We are fortunate to have strong communication with them and they feel comfortable with letting us know when we missed the mark.

Because we respect their opinions so much, we asked them for feedback and suggestions as we were developing ideas and writing this book. Josh and Sarah helped to organize a discussion group of their peers. We sought all their comments on the manuscript and found their suggestions to be extremely helpful, and their ideas are incorporated into the text. We can't thank them enough for their help and support.

There were a number of people who gave generously of their time and openly of their experience in our discussion groups. Their stories add a richness and reality to the book. Our heartfelt appreciation to Jed Bennett, Christine Carter, Mary Alice Copp, Daniel Fermaglich, Lois Fermaglich, Barry Fisher, Irene Fisher, Ellen Frohwirth, Vanessa Frohwirth, Kim Garabed, Carol Goodman, Lisa Hague, Bonnie Kazam, Ezra Kazam, Brett Kimmel, Blair MacInnes, Jane Rubinstein, Phil Rubinstein, Erika Salzman, Sondra Sen, Tapas Sen, Roslyn Stahl, Bonnie Weiss, Hannah Weiss, Richard Weiss, Adam Yellin and Michelle Zale.

Thank you to Barbara Scott, a special friend and wonderful mother of five young adults, who so generously provides us with a beautiful retreat where we are able to work on our books in comfort and privacy.

In our many years of practice, we have worked with numerous families who have struggled with many of the issues addressed in this book. We have learned from their stories – from what works and what hurts. We are honoured by their trust in us and in awe of the innate strength individuals have to work through difficult situations.

We want to acknowledge how much joy we experienced working on this book together. Through hours and hours of discussion, morning walks reviewing our ideas, poring over the manuscript page by page, we have both benefited and grown and learned from one another.

Finally, we are most appreciative of this opportunity to share our ideas with you, fellow parents and young adults wanting to strengthen your relationships with the important people in your life. Our thanks and good wishes to each of you.

Contents

Introduction

George, aged 26, recently moved back home with his parents for the second time since he finished college. He has already had two career changes and was recently laid off from a large corporation, the victim of a slow economy and downsizing. He has no immediate job prospects in his field. His parents were uneasy about having George home again. The last time was a disaster causing a lot of anger, which damaged their relationship.

Janney, aged 19, lives at home and is attending a local community college. Her parents expect her to have a part-time job, get good grades, keep to the same curfew she had in high school, and babysit her younger sister for three hours a day. All her friends have gone away to school. She is miserable and feels that her parents treat her like she is still 14 years old.

Dean and Dana were planning to redecorate their home and enjoyed retirement after their children had moved out and were settled in their own lives. One night they found Karen, aged 29, and her two children, aged two and four, on their doorstep. They needed a place to stay because Karen's husband had been arrested for embezzlement and their home was being seized. Karen moved back home, needing help with financial support as well as childcare until she could put her life back together. Dean and Dana found their plans turned upside down.

Tom, aged 25, has been living with a young woman of a different religion for two years. They plan to marry. Her parents refuse to speak to her since she has become involved in a relationship that is outside her faith. Tom hates to call his parents because all they do is criticize him.

These stories touch on some of the key dilemmas that might arise when our children become adults. We will focus in more detail on the issues raised by these young adults and their parents, examining options for dealing with them that are positive and supportive without being demeaning or intrusive. While every era has its own defining characteristics, the Generation Xers differ significantly from their parents and previous generations in many ways. As a result of moral, emotional, financial and occupational changes, parents are often frustrated, confused, even angry, in their interactions with their offspring. Adult children still turn to their parents for help and support, but too often feel infantilized or humiliated when their parents criticize them or tell them what to do.

Today, in the United States nearly 22 million adult sons and daughters are living in households maintained by one or both parents, compared with 1970, when only 15 million adult children lived with their families – a 46% increase. This represents a total of 15% of all families that include one or more children aged 18 or older. The increasing age at first marriage means that fewer young adults today are establishing their own household than was the case a generation ago. Continuing increases in the cost of establishing and maintaining a household may also mean that young adults today are not as well equipped financially to maintain a residence separate from their parents as they were in the 1970s. Many parents mistake their child's request for advice or help as a license to direct their life, and financial dependence can breed anger and resentment if it has too many strings attached. Moving back home can signal a regression in lifestyle for the parents and a regression in behavior for the adult child.

We felt compelled to write this book as there are more of our sons and daughters needing our help in some ways and because their generation is so different from ours in many areas. There are thousands of books offering advice on how to raise children until they reach 18 years of age. Very few books or chat shows reach out to parents of adult children, who are supposedly now grown up and present no more challenges. For us personally, this phase has been a time of soul-searching, questioning, sometimes hurt feelings, and often confusion. Parents want to help but are not always sure what is helpful. Our children ask for advice but don't really follow it. They want approval, but don't necessarily act in ways to garner approval. They may lack direction or change their minds, fall apart or plunge ahead. At the same time, we feel ourselves ageing, wanting to make changes, redefining ourselves.

Not only are there few books on this parenting phase, we found that friends are often reluctant to share problems and concerns. Parents seem more likely to offer good news than, for example, to acknowledge publicly that their child has a drinking problem. Perhaps we want to protect our child's privacy, not wanting friends or relatives to think less of our son or daughter. And perhaps, too, we want to protect our own image. After all, if our child is not becoming a perfect adult, aren't we responsible (at least that is the usual misperception)? It can be a lonely and difficult time.

As our three children entered their 20s, we found ourselves faced with new questions. In looking for guidance, we turned to friends and clients as well as our own children, listening to their struggles, learning from their resolutions, and developing a concept to help parents with adult children. We invited friends, clients, and our children's friends to discuss with us their thoughts about and experiences with the parent/young adult phase. We found an eagerness in the adult groups: a hunger to be able to talk freely in the anonymity of a focus group. What should I do? What are the rules? Am I helping too much? One parent even called it her 'dirty little secret' that she and her husband were subsidizing their 25-year-old son in an apartment.

What we propose in this book are not rules but a guiding philosophy to apply to the large variety of situations that arise with our adult children. We emphasize that this is a stage of many shifts taking place: a time of transition as our adult child tries to find his or her place in the world; a shift in the parent-child relationship; and a shift for us personally in our middle age. At this time we need to shift our parenting approach from the style we used when they were children. We need to shift from an authoritative, more directive approach to an indirect and supportive role.

During this phase in our parenting journey, our young adult offspring are experiencing a major transition in defining their lives while shifting in their perception of us, their parents. At the same time, we are experiencing shifts in our marriages, careers and lifestyles. We hope for an easier, more adult-to-adult relationship with our children at this stage, but what we often find is that we are still trying to have an authoritative parent-child relationship, which rarely works. Nor are we completely free of responsibility in our parenting when our sons and daughters continue to turn to us for advice and, sometimes, financial assistance.

We are writing this book as a conversation with parents and our adult children as we all continue to learn and refine our parent-child relationships. Our underlying premise is the concept of shifting from the role of a strong, controlling, authoritative figure to one of acceptance, friendship and support. The goal for parents at this stage is to maintain a close, positive relationship while encouraging our young adult children to grow and strengthen their independence throughout this difficult transitional period in their lives. We will suggest a number of options to deal with the variety of challenges that may occur, while stressing that there is no one rule or right approach. We can choose our options based on our family style, needs and resources, always keeping the focus on the positive role that parents can serve.

Throughout the book we will use the term 'young adult' to refer to our grown sons and daughters. The stories and examples presented are taken from a number of focus-group discussions held with parents and young adults, as well as examples from our own children's experiences and those of our friends and clients. With the exception of our children's stories, all names and circumstances have been altered to protect the individuals' privacy. We have included the thoughts and experiences of young adults who never left home after school and those who moved away and then returned home for a variety of reasons; young adults living on their own both with and without their parents' financial support. We offer vignettes of good parent-child relationships and alienated ones; parents who are married, widowed, divorced, financially secure and struggling. While we could not possibly include every individual situation, we have aimed for a representational cross section to illustrate the variety of challenges and the universality of experiences.

In each chapter or section, where appropriate, we have included questions or comments for you and your young adult to think about and discuss. These topics are meant as springboards to clarify your own ideas and encourage conversations to understand one another more fully, leading to a more satisfying relationship. You may find that your answers are different if your children are aged 18, 15 and 12 compared with those of families with three young adults. Your answers and responses may change throughout the years as your child ages and circumstances change. Our attitudes and behavior are influenced by the ages of our children, each young adult's personality and needs, and by the normal evolutionary process of life experiences.

While parenting is always a 'learn as you go' experience, dealing with our young adult children provoked more issues than anticipated. Adults in our focus discussion groups found it extremely helpful to share their concerns and to be validated by common experiences – clearly there is a need for more avenues of honest sharing among parents with older children. We hope this book will bring comfort in the commonality of experience, will enlighten you and inspire you to continue working on being more positive and supportive. Often after (and sometimes during) a conversation with one of our children, we remind each other to zip our lips, be non-judgmental, and not assume responsibility for their choices. It is an ongoing effort.

As we continue our parenting journey with our adult children, further shifts will occur and there will be times when we need our children to know us as whole people. Young adults have trouble with seeing parents as frail, infirm or needy. They are comfortable with seeing us in the role of providing for them, being available for them. This is one more example of the constantly evolving and changing relationship between parents and adult children.

While there are many issues that arise during this phase, it can also be a time of great joy, comfort and laughter. We learn to enjoy our children as people. If we can feel less responsible for their choices and focus more on their strengths, we can come together as special friends with a strong bond based on our shared history. Using the ideas and supportive approach suggested in this book, we can have many interactions that are pleasant, loving and life-enhancing.

Chapter 1

Profiles of young adults and their parents

Renee remembers, *'When I went away to college, I lived either in a dorm or sorority house [women's hall of residence] where there was an 11pm curfew during the week and a slightly later curfew at weekends. Dale and I were married one week after graduation when I was 21 years old. I got a full scholarship for graduate school [post-graduate college], which covered tuition plus additional spending money. Dale worked his way through college. His parents paid his medical school expenses but he donated blood and sat with patients on the midnight shift to earn his spending money. We rarely asked our parents for money or advice, and had two of our three children by the time I was 25.'*

In contrast, our three children have already travelled through more of the United States and abroad in their young lives than we have, and were financially supported through further education. Rebecca, our oldest, was very career-focused from the time she was 12 years old. She was married when she was 27 and had her first child at 30. Joshua has had several different careers and at one time moved to Colorado for a while to change his life before deciding to move back east. Sarah took a year off between college and graduate school to move to California and work at odd jobs. Although she is in a long-term relationship, she is in no hurry to get married.

What is this young adult generation all about? How did it get to be so different? For starters, when we were growing up, most families were intact, with one wage earner. For the majority, the father worked for the same company for a long time until he retired with a party and a gold watch for loyal service. Families had one television, a set dinner time, one phone line, and a lot of sharing and interdependence. Young adults in our generation expected to get a job immediately after completing their education. They had to earn money for a car and an apartment. There was a certain urgency to getting married in order to be together and have a sexual relationship.

Fast-forward 25 years and note the significant differences in behavior and cultural climate between young people today and the way our generation experienced this stage of development. This is the first generation to grow up entirely in a peacetime economy. It is also the first generation that may live a less affluent lifestyle than that of their parents. Today, in the majority of families both parents are working and the children are brought up with babysitters, daycare of some sort, or they are latchkey children left home alone. With the divorce rate stabilizing at about 50%, many children are shuffled back and forth between two homes. Out of guilt for their absence, parents are often lax with rules and responsibilities and overindulgent with material gifts. Many children grow up with an electronic heaven in their bedrooms: television, phone, computer, perhaps their own beeper.

The world has changed so rapidly that the prevalent attitude among young adults and their parents often seems to be one of confusion. So many young adults seem lacking in direction or plan. Parents wring their hands, trying to understand and cope with these adult offspring sitting at home unemployed, or wasting their time in jobs they don't really like. When we grew up, we had to have a plan, even if we changed the plan as we went along. We just jumped right in. That was the expectation. Now many of our children seem to expect to be taken care of while they leisurely take their time to move into full adult responsibilities.

One major change contributing to the confusion is in the workplace. Adults today feel themselves the victims of a fickle work environment, where maturity, experience and loyalty are no longer valued. Younger employees replace older employees because they are more up to date with technological advancements and can be paid less. An average worker today can expect to have at least eight different employers in the course of their adult life. In some cases, the employee will be made redundant. Other changes will be the result of the individual's choice. Not only will our young adults have a number of jobs, but the job market is rapidly changing. Occupations and positions exist today that weren't known five years ago and may be obsolete in a short time.

Social mores are looser and less defined. Children are sexually active at an incredibly early age, and in many parts of the US they may often be exposed to drugs and alcohol sometime before sixth grade (first year of secondary school). Neal Gabler in his 1999 book, *Life the Movie*, describes how entertainment values, characterized as 'fun, effortless, sensational, mindless, formulaic, predictable, and subversive', permeate every nook and cranny of American life. Movies, television and popular music extol easy sex, lack of commitment, violence and alienation. Without clear religious or moral guidelines, young people have easy access to sex and are therefore in no rush to get married.

While we were raised with the concept that adult life meant getting married, raising a family, getting a job with a good company and staying with that company until retirement, young people today want time to find themselves, find meaningful work, or put off joining the rat race for as long as possible. Parents now are confronted with behaviors we do not understand and questions for which there are no stock answers. Dale recalls, 'I think our parents – my parents – just parented. They emigrated from Europe, they didn't read books – they just did what they did and trusted that that was the best they could do. They didn't analyze. They worried about their kids but they didn't feel guilty. They just did whatever they did.' In many ways, life was simpler for our parents and for us.

One parent said, 'We are off the charts in terms of independence. We start in the early days of child rearing and when our child is 18, we turn around and can't understand why they aren't listening to us because everything in our culture pushes the independence theme. In other societies they teach interdependence, relying on other people, and it's a whole different expectation. Maybe the Japanese are too extreme in this respect, but we have gone too far in the opposite direction of independence and individualism. This "me" generation, who want to do their own thing, is too extreme.'

We call our children 'young adults' after the age of 18, but what is an adult today? The definition has always shifted over time. For hundreds of years in the Jewish tradition, a boy became a man at 13. In the first half of the last century, being an adult meant 'old enough to go to war'. One mother noted, 'Our children have all the privileges of adulthood at an early age, but they didn't earn them. They have sex in high school, their first apartment in college. They live like they are married – with mommy and daddy's support. It's like playing house.' Another parent noted that when his son was 19 and drove to Florida during spring break, he and his wife insisted that their son took a cell phone and called home several times a day so they wouldn't worry about him. Yet his own father at 19 was flying bombers over Germany. He added, 'I think our perception of being an adult is very different than it used to be. When you had to go to war, you were an adult. Now a 19-year-old can't take a road trip without a cell phone because the parents would worry. Maybe this society infantilizes kids forever. The whole idea of worrying about a 19-year-old – how old is a 19-year-old? Is he an adult or just a bigger kid?'

Perhaps nowhere is the difference between generations felt as dramatically as in immigrant sectors of the population. For example, young adult Hispanics, dubbed Generation Ñ (EN-yay), are finding their own cultural balancing act, living in two cultures at the same time.

Largely bilingual but more fluent in English than Spanish, they are entering their adult years with more demographic clout and education than their parents. For their parents, being Latino was a negative thing in the United States so they worked very hard to blend in. Young Latinos feel themselves 100% American but are comfortable enough to acknowledge their Latino roots. One poll showed that the majority of Latinos over the age of 35 identified themselves as American, while those under 35 identified themselves as Hispanic or Latino. As Generation Ñ grow in numbers and in influence, they tend to shift into ways that somewhat contradict their parents' patterns. With more second-generation children of immigrants coming into the workforce and with an increasing acceptance of ethnic, religious and racial intermarriage, we may expect more generational conflict.

One other important influence on the attitudes of young adults is the sociopolitical backdrop in which they have been raised. This generation tends to have great cynicism about the possibilities of a happy, long-term marriage. Fidelity is not something they have seen from parents or from many of their role models in the worlds of sports, arts, or politics. While not experiencing a war during their childhood, they have witnessed the ever-present tensions in the Middle East, Ireland, and other parts of the world, terrorism both abroad and at home, violence in the news and in the media, and our political leaders exposed for immoral behaviors.

Feelings of displacement

For a variety of reasons, some young adults may experience feelings of displacement. Often when a young adult moves out or goes to college, a younger sibling will move into their room. For the sibling, that room may represent a chance to have their own space or to get the 'prize' – the bigger room. But for the young adult returning home, even for a short visit, it can be disconcerting when your personal space no longer exists.

This displacement also occurs when the parents move to a different home. In either situation, your childhood domain has disappeared. Renee's parents moved when she was newly married. She recalls, 'The new home was lovely but it had only the master bedroom and a guestroom. I was going home, but not really – indeed I felt like the guest. It was not my home. I didn't know where to find things and there wasn't a trace of my personal belongings. Books, furniture, knick-knacks had all been sold or packed away.'

We associate home with a certain familiarity and comfort level, which is still important to a young adult for many years, probably until they feel well established with roots in their own family, home and community. That doesn't mean we should never give younger siblings a better room or move, if that is in our best interest. It only suggests we need to understand and be aware of these possible feelings.

Another kind of displacement occurs when a divorced or widowed parent remarries. The young adult's home may be the same physical structure but it takes on a feeling of being invaded if a step-parent and their children move in. The tone of the family as well as the physical space is significantly changed, and it may take a while for the young adult to adjust. As we will stress throughout the book, the key to weathering these shifts is to understand their feelings and be able to talk things over in a non-blaming, tolerant and loving way.

Attitudes about work

In terms of finding work and/or a career path, young adults have ambivalent feelings and have received mixed messages from parents while growing up. Peter feels that many adults consider this generation to be lazy. He believes they are not so much lazy as professing a different work ethic than their parents possess. His parents stressed the importance of getting good grades to go to a top college from the time he was in elementary school. Once he was in college, they encouraged him to take whatever courses he wanted and really enjoy this special time in his life. For three and a half years, he was told to enjoy himself. Then as graduation approached, the message shifted to 'Hurry up and decide what you are going to do.' A record number of college students are taking more than four years to graduate because they change their major and are in no hurry to enter the 'real world'.

George elaborates further: 'I could say we're lazy, but we're not. We're a little more liberal and we kind of... I don't know, it's hard to explain. We're encouraged to be freethinkers and explore, and do what we want, yet at the same time we have to have a job and we have to be doing something.' Most of the young adults we heard from stress the importance of having a job they liked. They have a somewhat idealistic view of work, wanting it to be meaningful and satisfying, a job they look forward to every day. They grew up watching parents work long hours and come home exhausted and irritable, with little time for family interaction. Many young adults don't want that kind of lifestyle and they accept the reality that they may not be able to afford the same material comforts with which they grew up.

In another discussion, Walter said, 'To find a job that you're satisfied with and enjoy doing – it's not going to happen. So I also have a negative view about work in that I just have a very difficult time envisioning being happy in a job – really feeling passionate about what I'm doing for a living. That would be fantastic, but I really can't envision that in any way, shape or form. I work because I have to pay the bills.'

We asked if this notion that work is work and it's not supposed to be pleasant – so as long as you get your money, it's okay – is something their parents gave them?

Janice replied, 'Yeah, I'm trying to break away from my parents' ideas about work and just try to create my own experience because my father is more like the hard-core businessman. You get money and you can buy nice things, and have the lifestyle you want. He tells me it doesn't matter that everyone's political and two-faced, you just do what you have to do and then you'll make more money. I don't agree with that. So many people complain about work. Right now I'm trying to establish my own beliefs about it and have faith, but I really don't see it. It's hard for me to break away from those beliefs because there are so few people who are happy with what they do.'

The job issue is complicated by the plethora of newly created jobs and opportunities, the lack of specific training for vocational or career paths, the desire of young adults to be happy in their work life, and the general unwillingness to work 60 to 70 hours a week to advance up the corporate ladder. Some young people almost scorn a materialistically driven work life, while others as a product of this lifestyle find themselves working just as hard or even harder than their parents. Many employers expect employees to work ridiculously long hours, holding them captive to the threat of downsizing and reorganizing.

Attitudes about marriage

Since 1960 in the United States the number of women marrying in any given year has declined by more than 40%, while the number of cohabiting couples has increased ten-fold during the same period to 4.3 million couples in 1998. The percentage of married couples who said they were 'very happy' has also dropped considerably from 53.5% in 1973 to only 37.8% in 1996 according to one study. Although the divorce rates appear to have stabilized at around 50%, young people are increasingly skeptical about having a satisfying long-term marriage.

As a result, more men and women are getting married at a later age than ever before. The U.S. Census Bureau reported that in 1997 the median age for men at first marriage was 26.7, and for women it was 25. In my day, if you weren't married by 21 or 22, you were already labeled an old maid. Today's young adults seem in no hurry. Perhaps as a result of the women's movement in the 1970s, women are now more comfortable with being on their own and having a career. Janice, aged 28, explains: 'It's comforting to know that I'm capable of holding a full-time job and supporting myself because I don't know if my ideal is going to happen – if I'm going to get married and have kids, and not have to work. Maybe it's not going to happen so it's good to know that I can support myself, and that I do have an education.' Amy, 19 and a college freshman, adds, 'You talk to girls at my college. "Yeah, I'm getting married at 27 and I'll have kids by 35," they say. But there are so many things that can happen in between. I want to focus on college right now and get good grades. I want to figure out my career first before I decide about kids and all that.'

Bill, 24, has been in a serious relationship for five years. His mother pressures him to get engaged but he states adamantly, 'I'm not too young to get married. My life is too young to get married!' Young adults all have concerns that they will have a good marriage. Walter questions, 'How will I know? My parents got divorced after 24 years. It really makes me nervous. How am I going to know if that is the right person because my parents thought they knew once? I think I know, but then I don't think I know anymore. Forget about unconditional love. I have unconditional doubt!'

If young women were to get married, they have mixed opinions about the question of whether they would be a home-based mom or have a career. They have grown up with the dual expectations to raise a family and have a job outside the home. Renee remembers, 'In the late '60s and '70s I was criticized by peers for choosing to work while our children were growing up. Often those women who have a deep commitment to or love of their jobs choose the career path. Once on a career path, where you have a taste of moving up the corporate ladder with more financial remuneration, success and power, it becomes part of your identity and thus harder to forgo. However, for women working just to pay the bills, the desire to be able to stay home with the children may be greater.'

Unlike previous generations, more young adults express comfort with the choice not to have children. They are not interested in giving up their lifestyle and perceived freedoms to take on the responsibilities of parenthood. Previous generations may have felt that way, but that would have been viewed by society as a selfish option. Today, young adults seem accepting of this choice, although their parents may express disappointment at missing the grandparent experience.

Younger Hispanic women are rejecting the traditional roles of their parents. Elena notes that in her parents' marriage her father is definitely the head of the house. 'He makes the decisions and that's how it is. Women today want to be treated as equal partners, and we are less tolerant of a machismo attitude, of cheating, and of waiting on our man.' In previous generations the women lived at home until they married. As young Latino women raised with an American attitude, many want to taste their freedom, move out, be independent, work for a while. These young women are more likely than their mothers to date and marry outside their community.

The role of organized religion

For most of the young adults with whom we spoke, religion meant little more than the obligatory appearance during holidays. When asked what role, if any, religion played in her life at this age, Amy replied, 'It doesn't play a role in my life. I was brought up Catholic and went to Sunday school, took Holy Communion, was confirmed, and the whole nine yards. But my parents (and I'm thankful to them for this) left it up to us after we were confirmed whether we wanted to continue going to church and practice that religion. I opted not to. I don't go to church every Sunday. I don't agree with a lot of the rules and values of the religion.' Bill had a slightly different upbringing with similar results: 'My father was Jewish, my mother was Catholic. I went to the Lutheran church just because it was around the corner. My parents never pushed me but I went alone from the time I was nine years old until I was 17, which is kind of weird. But then I just decided I wasn't into organized religion. There are things that make sense and things that don't make sense.'

Debbie described a different experience, 'Religion to me was going to CCD and hating it as a kid, even though it was only two hours. Holy Communion was fun because you have a party. Then it came time for confirmation and I was 16, and becoming an adult. I thought I was becoming Miss Independent. I didn't want to be confirmed. I didn't want to be in the Catholic religion – I didn't like what they believe in. I have a godmother who's Unitarian and I went to one of her services and fell in love with religion. I thought, this is so good. They believe in unity. But my mom still made me get confirmed. Then something happened to me recently and something just snapped, and I said to my mom, "We're going to church." And ever since I've been going to church, and that was about a year and a half ago. Every Sunday, God's become a big part of my life. I've become more religious since that day. It helps me get through things.'

Many Latino young adults are struggling with their religious beliefs. While overwhelmingly Roman Catholic, they consider their religion to be more of a cultural inheritance than an obligation. Growing up in Latin American countries, where poverty and hardship are the norm, religion was a comfort and a community mainstay. With more affluence and opportunities, these Latino adults now feel freer to question or move away from some religious practices.

Walter came from a mixed marriage, where his dad was Jewish and his mom was Catholic. They celebrated Christmas but not the Jewish holidays. He went to Hebrew school but had very little religious training in the home. 'I think that combination sort of put me in neutral for a while,' he said. 'I identify with being Jewish, although to Jewish people I'm not technically Jewish and I'm not technically a Catholic, so I'm sort of in the middle. But I decided to make my connection to Judaism, but in all honesty I don't really think about it much. I'd like to learn a little bit more about it, but I really won't take action on it until I have children. The only thing that I'm very, very serious about is that my kids are brought up Jewish. That will never change, though I don't know why I feel so strongly about this as I'm not dead set on most things.'

In general, young adults didn't talk much about a spiritual point of view. Our son, Josh, expressed his surprise that not one young adult mentioned the goal of being a good person. When asked what they thought was really important in life, several answered in agreement with Janice: 'I think for me I'd say inner peace is the most important thing that I could ever find. Nothing materialistic or concrete could ever be as powerful, I don't think, as the abstract internal contentment with oneself. I think I might have high expectations for that to happen but that's what's important to me.'

Debbie reflected a point of view affected by her childhood experiences: 'Actually I was thinking about this and feeling scared because of my parents' divorce. To me, avoiding any lifetime commitment until I find happiness and peace of mind is important because I still feel like it's more trial and error. I almost feel like my parents struggled, they got married and then had me – it pushes the happiness to wait even further. Unless, of course, they were happy once, but then they weren't... So I think happiness is important, especially before you make major commitments.' Walter seconded that concept: 'I was going to say one word – happiness. The main thing is to be happy with yourself. Everyone knows that. Money to me is very important but money doesn't bring happiness. It helps to get by but it's not the most important thing.' The Dalai Lama has often suggested that all beings are seeking happiness. It is the purpose of life.

Wanting a positive relationship with parents

Everyone stresses the importance of a good relationship with his or her parents. Many struggle with feelings of rejection and stress in their relationships with parents but they seem ever hopeful that it might get better or that they could one day actually win the approval of their parents. One young woman summed it up by saying, 'What I really want is to have peace between me and my parents because at this point it doesn't look like it's going to happen anytime soon. I have a daddy, not a father, and I have a mother, not a mommy, if you can understand that concept. All my friends have dads. Mine only talks about his social life and asks superficially if everything is okay. Not that I want to be hearing lectures from my father. And I've got a mother who only wants to know "Did you pay your bills?" "Did you do this?" "I'm okay mom," I tell her. I called her to tell her I was sick and she said, "Did you pay your Visa bill?" "Okay, bye mom". Those are the relationships I have. I have two opposites and I just pray that God will one day let me have peace and have a happy norm between both of them.'

We were struck by the longing of these young people, no matter what their ages, to have a warm and supportive relationship with their parents at this time in their life. Developing both a strong sense of your own identity and a friendly relationship with parents gives our young adult a sense of a strong central core and enhanced inner resources to deal with life's challenges.

Attitudes toward health, AIDS and STDs

One other area of importance is the impact of AIDS and sexually transmitted diseases in the lives of socially active young adults. Without exception, they seemed uniformly naive and misinformed, all the while thinking they knew a great deal about it. They are extremely trusting that if they meet someone at work or through friends and they seem like a nice person with a good job, there is no need to worry or take precautions against AIDS or STDs. Their almost careless attitude toward this crucial health issue is in sharp contrast to the obsession with exercising and being healthy. They have grown up with the cultural messages to be slim, eat low-fat food and work out. While they seem almost narcissistically involved in their appearance, they are only casually interested in protecting themselves from serious sexually transmitted diseases.

Visions for the future

Parents of young adults, while confused by some of their choices and lifestyle, generally have a vision that their adult sons and daughters will lead valuable, productive lives. One parent noted that she just trusts her children are going to get where they need to be. 'You trust that they're going to make it. Somewhere down the road – one year, two years, five years – they're going to do what they need to do. I think our kids will be okay. Some will be happier than others. I don't know what kind of lifestyles they are going to evolve for themselves, but I think they're going to put their feet on the ground. I think they are basically great kids with a great set of values who just need to grow up some more.'

Many young adults with whom we have talked have confusion about the future. One young woman noted that for someone like her sister, who knew she wanted to be a doctor from an early age, life is easier. She reiterated a comment we heard from many: 'If you have a goal, you have a vision about where you are going. But if you don't know what you really want to do, it is hard to have a direction for the future. It seems that life is only about struggling and then you die. What's the point?' There is a certain cynicism and underlying depression for many young adults.

As our young people are evolving in determining the direction for themselves, many parents at this stage also seem to be redefining themselves. Many women feel free to take up a new career or business once the youngest child leaves home. Although experiencing sadness at the end of their active parenting phase, they look forward to the shift with increasing freedom to focus on themselves and their own needs. There also tends to be a high rate of divorce among couples married for 20 to 25 years, as if their children were the glue holding them together and once the children moved into independence, the parents did not have enough of a bond together to make it work. Often couples sell the family home to move into separate apartments or a smaller condo, removing traces of their children's childhood. For the marriages that continue, couples often start to enjoy having more personal time together and begin to think of retiring.

There may also be a shift in our role vis-à-vis our elderly parents, finding that we now take on the role of caretaker and thus have to parent our parents. The demands of infirm parents can be extremely stressful as is the loss of your parents, no matter what our age. Nonetheless, this stage of life is ripe with possibilities and opportunities: our children blossoming as they find direction and adventures, and ourselves shifting into new paths as well. All the more reason to strengthen the bonds of friendship, trust and respect with our sons and daughters.

Chapter 2

Redefining and nurturing the relationship based on respect and enjoyment, not dependence

The cocoon

A man found a cocoon of a butterfly.

One day a small opening appeared. He sat and watched the butterfly for several hours as it struggled to force its body through that little hole. Then it seemed to stop making any progress. It appeared as if it had gotten as far as it could and it could go no further. Then the man decided to help the butterfly, so he took a pair of scissors and snipped off the remaining bit of the cocoon.

The butterfly emerged easily.

But it had a swollen body, and small shrivelled wings. The man continued to watch the butterfly because he expected that, at any moment, the wings would enlarge and expand to be able to support the body, which would contract in time. Neither happened! In fact, the butterfly spent the rest of its life crawling around with a swollen body and shrivelled wings.

It was never able to fly.

What the man in his kindness and haste did not understand was that the restricting cocoon and the struggle required for the butterfly to get through the tiny opening were God's way of forcing fluid from the body of the butterfly into its wings so that it would be ready for flight once it achieved its freedom from the cocoon. Sometimes struggles are exactly what we need in our life. If God allowed us to go through our life without any obstacles, it would cripple us. We would not be as strong as we could have been.

And we could never fly.

Author unknown

It goes without saying that we all want to have a good relationship. Young adults want to be viewed as older, more mature, independent and capable than when they were in high school. They want their parents' support and unconditional love along with the freedom to make their own choices. As parents we are looking to feel comfortable with our children, although we may still feel the need to tell them what to do. Our sense of wanting to protect them from poor choices needs to shift at this stage in our parenting relationship. We can take a backseat role as adviser, allowing them to make choices, maybe even mistakes (in our opinion). It's crucial that we acknowledge the fact that we really don't understand their world to a great extent. We also don't always know what is best for our individual child, much as we might like to consider ourselves experts.

Creating space and building respect

The relationship with our young adults may be partially dependent on what took place as they were growing up. One parent noted, 'I think the relationship with older kids is just a continuation of relationships with younger kids – it doesn't change because they are older. It modifies, but if you didn't get along and the kids didn't respect you when they were 10, it's not going to happen when they are 20. If you didn't enjoy being with them when they were 10, you don't want to be with them when they are older, so it's an extension of what was going on those years before.' Although relationships do build on previous experience, they are constantly changing and shifting as we grow and our children mature. We don't have to be pessimistic. In fact, it is essential to be optimistic. Human relationships are dynamic. They are always changing. At times we move closer together, at times there is distance.

The relationship often changes as our children leave home to go away to school or to live on their own. Gloria noticed, 'I've developed a better relationship with my parents and understand them more now that I'm older and more independent. It's not that I wasn't able to be free and do as I pleased while I lived at home as an adult, but I felt stifled. Regardless of how much space I was given or freedom to do what I wanted, I definitely felt stifled. It's nothing against my parents, I just think it just gets to a point where it's inevitable that you are going to feel stifled and so you have to break away. I talk to them daily and see them at least once or twice a week, so we do stay in touch.'

Walter agreed: 'I like having a little space because when we talk on the phone, it's easier for me to say I disagree. You come to the realization that your parents are not always right.' Gloria continued as we discussed an area where she and her parents definitely disagree. 'These issues are difficult but because I'm on my own and fairly independent now, it's easier to know that my views on things are okay, that this is the way our age bracket is going. It just seems like it's easier to feel that parents are right when you live at home – it's their house. But when you are living on your own, you can feel freer to question those beliefs.'

Both parents and young adults agreed that a healthy relationship depends on mutual respect. One parent commented that 'respect and love are really very important, but of the two, I think that respect is more important. I think love just comes with closeness. Respect is something that you have to earn and you also have to demand. I tell parents they have to respect themselves and their children have to give them respect.' As our children mature, it may be hard for us to listen to a difference in opinion and not view it as being disrespectful.

Respect is earned by acting with dignity and kindness. Fran told this story: 'I have a friend who came from a very loving close family, like I think all of ours are, but when she turned 18 she found out that her dad had been having an affair for two years. It totally reshaped their entire family and nobody is close anymore. It's changed her whole view of the world. It's just very upsetting and her relationship with her father – well, she has none. Her relationship with her mother has also totally changed. They used to be very close and she respected her mother's opinion. Now she just goes about her own thing, she does whatever. She thinks her growing-up years were all a lie. Her parents split when she went to college and from then on it's deteriorated, and it's very sad because they were known in the town as a certain kind of family and when this got out, it was a huge thing. It put a big burden on the children, because they thought they had one kind of family and really they had another.'

Adult children at the younger end of the spectrum are perhaps more likely to move away than their older peers. In the late teens and early 20s, young adults are struggling to establish an identity. They often feel a need to separate themselves from parents in a variety of ways. If living at home, they may retreat to their room, seeming withdrawn from the rest of the family. They still want to proclaim their individuality by their dress, choice of music and friends. They may feel the need to be argumentative. It can be an awkward time in terms of family rules and expectations, which will be addressed in detail in chapter three – Living arrangements. Students in their last year of high school often experience what we called Senioritis. It is a kind of push-pull attitude toward their family, especially mom and dad. While they proclaim their eagerness to 'get out', they become irritable and moody, as if also regretting their imminent leap into adulthood. At other times, students may choose to spend more time hanging out with the folks and less time with friends. And they begin to find a greater appreciation for their parents. For Mother's Day during his senior year (upper sixth), our nephew gave his mother an arrangement of yellow roses and a beautiful card. His mom was shocked. She had never received so much as a comment from her son in previous years. On the other hand, when young adults criticize their parents' attitudes or interests, it may be part of their attempt to distance themselves. At some later age, they may in fact identify with or come to enjoy those same interests.

As our children get older, they may experience living away from home at some point. Even if they move back home, they are on their way to an awareness of being separate, of being an adult. This awareness is a key component as we redefine our relationship. The more our young adult seems settled – has a secure job with a steady income, develops a comfortable social network and a positive sense of self – the less we feel the need to offer advice and the freer they may feel to enjoy our company.

What we hope to create is a special kind of parent-offspring friendship. We want to look forward to spending time with our young adults, whether it's part of a family gathering, holiday event or casually hanging out. As with everything in life, there is a delicate balance we each have to find and maintain. All three of our children presently live within 45 minutes to one hour away (without traffic). Two of our children have complained at times that they feel neglected, that we are too busy to see them. The third feels we see each other a little too much. We see them roughly the same amount, about twice a month, and talk to them one to three times a week on the phone, depending on what's happening.

When our young adult needs to create distance, either physically by being less present or by criticizing our beliefs, the key to maintaining our relationship is to become less controlling in how we love our son or daughter. The idea is not to cut off the relationship when they don't do what we want them to do. By being tolerant and accepting of their need to find their own way, by letting go of our tight control, our young adult will actually feel more connected. In the Buddhist view, separation and connectedness exist simultaneously. One makes the other possible. Connection is our natural state; we just have to learn to accept the duality of its nature.

Our relationship with our growing child can be likened to that between a crew and a deep-sea diver. The crew maintains the operating base, keeping the boat steady and available. The diver goes off into unknown territories to explore, maintaining a vital connection to the crew. In case of emergency or at periodic intervals, the diver returns to the boat for nourishment, rest and further direction. The crew and the diver are interdependent. The diver cannot safely explore without the security of a reliable crew, and the crew on the boat cannot complete their mission without the diver's explorations.

Unlike the deep-sea diver, however, families have no instructions on when and how to let go. The lack of a training manual is only one reason that parenting is such a challenge. As parents we need to trust our own capacity to let go, listening to our instincts and being sensitive to our young adult's behavior. We also need to learn to trust their ability to be separate. Each family needs to find its own unique path in developing a stronger bond with their child at this stage.

Gloria, aged 29, mentioned earlier that she sees her parents once or twice a week. She lives only 15 minutes away in her own apartment but likes to stop over to chat, borrow one of her sister's outfits and have a good meal. Each family has to define its own balance. It is important not to take it personally if our son or daughter isn't so eager to see us, especially if we trust the relationship to be basically strong. Rather we can feel pleased that their life is so full, we don't have to fill in the empty spaces. Hopefully, if any of us wants more time together or more distance, the lines of communication are strong enough to allow honest discussion of our needs. We can say something like, 'I'm missing you. Let's check our calendars and find a date to get together for dinner sometime soon'. This sounds so much more inviting that an angry 'Why haven't you called?' or a complaining 'I never hear from you unless you want something'.

Some of the parents we interviewed mentioned being intimidated by their children. We might be intimidated by the younger generation's comfort level in arguing and speaking their mind. Children say things to us that we hardly dared to think, let alone express directly to our parents. As Renee explains, 'I got punished if I argued about a curfew or any other topic with my parents, whereas today's teen might follow a parent around the house and badger until they get the curfew they want.'

While our children have learned to be very assertive, I think sometimes we parents have been too quick to back down. Perhaps we equated being loved and having a good relationship with giving in. One parent commented, 'We are terribly indulgent and we think about our kids' psyches way too much.' Joan worries, 'I look at my sister, who is younger than me and had her children late in life. I see the difference in how I raised my kids and how she is raising hers. I look at her children and wonder how they are going to go out into the world. They think the world revolves around them. They are totally sheltered. My sister asks them, "Do you want to go to bed now?" instead of announcing their bedtime.' With our adult children, it is a tricky balance between expressing our opinion and being overbearing or dogmatic. Let's look at some keys to strengthening our communication.

Improving communication

Some parents hesitate to talk to their young adults for fear that they will be perceived as meddling or too nosy. Following is an illustrative discussion from one group of parents:

Dorothy: *I'd be happy to advise my adult children, except they don't want my advice and they don't ask for it so it's a moot point.*

Terri: *I really try very, very hard not to give advice. I'm reminded of and amused by the expression 'Bite your tongue' because sometimes that's literally what it takes, so I take that phrase very seriously.*

Renee: *Only now you can change it to 'Zip your lips'.*

Tad: *But don't you still try to guide them a little?*

Elise: *Tina perceived me as much too controlling when she was younger so now I am very careful to say nothing. If she were to ask my opinion, I would tell her but she doesn't ask so I really try to keep my mouth shut and just be encouraging of the things that she's doing that I think are great. While she was at college we didn't have any controls on her, but I think she has carried that fierce feeling of wanting independence. Now she's finally beginning to realize that there's no need to rebel. It's taken her a long time to relax and realize that she is a free agent, that she can let her guard down and not be so fearful that we're going to try to steer her.*

Terri: *I really resent what I would call the subjugation of my natural instincts in order to play out this little dance that Elise is talking about. I have to repress and change my instincts to accommodate the relationship. I know it's right and it's better but there are times...*

Dorothy: *I think what our kids resent most are the questions. First of all I always find it's a better conversation if they call us rather than me calling them.*

Terri: *The questions... Sometimes I learned if I treat subjects with humor, I can get away with much more. But sometimes I don't care how I phrase something, they still hear it as 'You idiot'.*

We included this story in our book, *Zip Your Lips: The Parents' Guide to*

Brief and Effective Communication, and it bears repeating. Dale had a young woman come to see him who tearfully began the session by saying, 'I hate my parents so much.' As the tears rolled down her cheeks, she explained that she had a good job, her own apartment and was supporting herself. She was excited to tell her parents that she had purchased a kitten to keep her company and make her apartment feel more homely. Her parents reacted by berating her: 'Why did you do that? It's stupid. Shots and food cost money, and you are barely making enough to pay your bills. You won't even be home to take care of it. You don't need a kitten, you need a boyfriend.' As they continued to tell her what a poor decision she had made, she felt angry and demeaned.

Several days later, our 25-year-old son called from his apartment to share his good news. He had gone to an animal shelter and 'saved the life' of a small kitten. Our first reaction might have been to criticize him, much as the young woman's parents just described had done. However, with the benefit of that recent experience, we said only, 'That's great.' We were able to share his enthusiasm so that he felt pleased about the conversation. While it may not have seemed like a good idea to us (the practical parents), the cat has turned out to be a loving companion, a source of entertainment and an opportunity for Josh to practice responsibility for another.

As you know, there are situations where a child's decision does not turn out for the best. On those occasions our children especially need our support and our silence. The consequence itself provides an opportunity for growth and learning. As parents, our role is to support that learning and our young adult's ability to handle it. 'I told you so' types of statements simply rub salt into the wound. Once a child's decision has been made or an action has occurred, the best response is silence. Allow children to experience the consequences of their own choices instead of saying, 'I told you so.' Zip your lips. Silence encourages more positive feelings from your child and frees them to learn from the experience.

Debbie talks about another kind of silent response: 'Maybe it's really important for parents to hear that we want them to listen. Just listen. Parents want to fix all their children's problems. They tell us what to do, but they have to realize that the child's mind changes. Even in eighth grade [at 13] or in high school, it's still different than when you were 10 years old. We want our parents to just listen. Be that shoulder to cry on, just be someone to give a really good hug when we need one.'

In nurturing our relationship there are numerous opportunities to zip our lips. When our young adults ask specifically for our advice and we feel strongly about an issue, we can express our ideas but without judgment. That is another key to a strong relationship. Noelle, aged 22, lives at home. She has a full-time job and an active social life. She describes her relationship with her mother as very difficult. 'Shouldn't your mother be on your side?' she asked tearfully. It seems if she decides not to continue a relationship, her mother sides with the young man, calling her selfish, too demanding and telling Noelle she is so hateful that no one will ever want to marry her. Before Noelle leaves the house on a date, her mother criticizes her clothes, her makeup, her hair, often telling her she looks like a slut.

Emily has a similarly negative relationship with her father. 'Growing up, I could never please him. Whatever I did, it wasn't good enough. If I got an A– he angrily asked why it wasn't an A.' Recently her parents traveled several hundred miles to visit her for Easter weekend. She took care to prepare a very special gourmet meal, which she had previously fixed to rave reviews from friends. Her father took a few bites of roasted quail and commented, 'I'd give this a C+.' Emily was devastated and, needless to say, will not look forward to the next visit.

Elise, suffering from a severe case of fibromyalgia, had been feeling some hostility and tension in her relationship with her daughter, Tina. Elise describes a conversation that allowed them to clear the air: 'This year I had some experiences with Tina that were confusing. It seemed like she would be so irritable when I called her on the phone and she would be rushing off somewhere. The periods between phone calls seemed longer and longer, and I had a feeling she was mad at me for being sick. She didn't really want to know I was sick. So that was painful and then we met at my mother's house in Florida in the spring. I was trying to make everything nice and act like I was healthier than I was, just so I wouldn't worry her. It was this business of trying to accommodate all the time to make everything be all right, and it seemed like the more I did, the pricklier she got.

'Finally one day I just had had it. She was short with me and there was no need, so I said let's go in the bedroom, I'd really like to talk. We went in and I told her how I felt. I didn't understand why she was being so cross with me and wondered what was her problem? She burst into tears and said she'd had all this guilt for how she'd been prickly with me the preceding couple of years. We then had the best talk we'd had in a long, long time and all this stuff poured out – how she was mad at me for letting her abuse me all these years and although the abuse has been rather subtle, it was this constant irritability with me every time I would express an opinion about anything. It was so fascinating. She asked me to tell her when she's out of line. She said this had come up in her own relationship because her boyfriend is a very kind, giving person and I could see where she could just mow him right down. She doesn't want to do that, she really values him. She wants to be told when she's acting selfish because she really doesn't want to be that way.

'We set up new ground rules. I've been the super-accommodating person out of my fear of losing her or alienating her and she's been this prickly person because she's been wanting to get away with it but on the other hand wanting me to pull her up on it. Since we established the new ground rules she's been trying to be more careful. So when she came home for Christmas and I asked her to go out to lunch with me (I have invited her to go to the movies or lunch for years and it's always been a polite turndown) she went out to lunch with me. She seemed delighted and so was I.'

Our young adults look to us for boundaries as well as unconditional love and support. In this difficult transitional stage, we may be the one source of comfort or encouragement. Our words have the power to wound deeply or to uplift. Obviously we will have a more enjoyable relationship with our young adult if they feel uplifted in our presence. Often when they ask for advice, they may already know their preference. They ask, not out of true curiosity but usually out of the need for validation. Josh was trying to decide between several job offers. He asked if he could come home to talk with us about his options. We had been listening to the same material for several weeks during a series of phone calls, so we didn't know what new information Josh might have. Nor could we really form an opinion as to the best job opportunity for him. We felt that he was in a much better position to understand the corporate world and determine the next move for his career path than we were. Nevertheless he presented the various possibilities. We listened and asked for clarification on specific details. When he was finished, he looked very relieved and said, 'So you agree with me I should accept the first offer?' We had taken care not to indicate any preference, but in hearing himself out, he arrived at his own conclusion and then wanted us to okay his choice.

We have all had the experience of a child asking our opinion. Rebecca showed us two evening dresses she bought for a fancy business occasion and asked which one she should keep. We commented that we liked the blue one. She answered that she really preferred the gray and asked if it would be appropriate for this particular party. She knew her preference. She needed us only to make her feel comfortable about her choice. We need to encourage our children to trust their own instincts, not to rely on ours or anyone else's. This is empowering and nurtures a positive relationship.

Joan shares this experience: 'Talking about shifting things, I do think it makes a difference how much advice you give because, as I said, this one daughter, she's already 35 years old, lives in Chicago and would call me almost every day and ask if she should turn on the water for whenever. And then I realized, of course, she was becoming more and more resentful of me because I was giving her advice. What she really wanted me to say was "You can figure it out" but I remained the mom, telling her what to do. At her age, she was having an adolescent rebellion against me completely and utterly. I thought we had the perfect mother-daughter relationship. I want to tell you I thought that because we talked all the time. We had a lot of fun, she was humorous, but it just all broke loose and this was mainly because she was basically too dependent on me. Once I realized what was happening and I pulled back, she started to make choices more independently and our relationship seemed to improve.'

Some of you may already be asking, but what if you really don't like their choice? Or what if their decision might be self-destructive? When there is no potential for harm, you can offer your opinion in a neutral tone of voice, or throw out a few concerns for your young adult to think about. For example, if Josh had received one job offer with higher pay that included very long workdays, we might have asked him if he had considered the impact on his life of working such long hours. With Rebecca we might have wondered whether the gray dress was too tight or too casual for the occasion. Comments like these serve to get across your opinion without demeaning your young adult. The feeling tone in wondering if the dress is too tight is very different from saying, 'You look terrible in the gray dress. It's much too tight and makes you look fat.' The latter response, in essence, is telling her, 'You don't know what you are doing', and attacking her personally.

We need to trust ourselves as parents, to remember that we put a lot of effort into raising our child. We gave them guidance and advice – now it's their time to try their own wings. Since we are smart but not omnipotent, there are innumerable situations where we might have handled a situation differently but our young adult's choice worked for them. So part of redefining and nurturing the relationship is to trust the job we have already done, trust our child to learn and make choices, and know that they will grow from all kinds of experiences, including those where the decision will not work out so well. Some examples of statements that are supportive are:

- 'That's just my opinion.'
- 'You'll figure it out.'
- 'You know what is best.'
- To remind our young adult of a past experience when they felt indecisive but came to a resolution and it worked out well.

Resolving conflicts

Anger, family turmoil, misunderstandings and conflicts are a natural part of every relationship. We cannot eliminate or totally avoid conflict. We can learn appropriate ways to resolve issues, being loving and effective in order to promote growth and change.

There are times when we inadvertently hurt our young adult's feelings. One such incident happened over a birthday party. The details are irrelevant because it has to do with perceptions. As a result of our daughter's perception that we were angry with her, at the end of a family party she told us that we had ruined the party for her and for everyone there. She left in tears and left Renee stunned and also in tears. We talked it over, reviewing the details, and tried to decide how to handle it. Renee called her the next morning to tell her she was sorry she was so upset, that it had not been our intent to hurt her. She also said that in a family with so much love, we could work out any disagreements. Our daughter told us she wasn't ready to talk about it but thanked us for calling.

She called the next day and we each shared our perceptions of what happened. We talked again later that week and eventually it smoothed over. The resolution was not to prove that one person was to blame. Rather we tried to understand one another's viewpoint, and agree we both felt sad for hurting each other.

In resolving family conflict, it is crucial to invite discussion of the issue. We need to respect each person's right to talk without interruption and to show receptive attention. That means to fully listen with an intent to understand what is being explained. When we are listening only for a pause so we might insert our defense or rebuttal, we are not really listening. There is a time to talk and a time to listen. This is not a courtroom and we do not want to act like a prosecuting attorney trying to prove the defendant (in this case, our son or daughter) wrong or bad. That is the opposite of a healing approach.

There is also a time to apologize. We can serve as a role model in accepting our responsibility in a conflict. Perhaps we spoke too harshly, made an erroneous assumption, or forgot to do something. Maybe we simply hurt our young adult's feelings without meaning to do so. An apology means we own our part of the interaction. It can move the resolution forward toward reconciliation. There are two poems that speak of resolving conflicts:

The Tone of Voice

It's not so much what you say
As the manner in which you say it;
It's not so much the language you use
As the tone in which you convey it;
"Come here!" I sharply said,
And the child cowered and wept.
"Come here," I said –
And straight to my lap he crept.

Words may be fair
And the tone may pierce like a dart;
Words may be soft as the summer air
But the tone may break my heart;
For words come from the mind
Grow by study and art –
But tone leaps from the inner self
Revealing the state of the heart.
Whether you know it or not,
Whether you're mean or care,
Gentleness, kindness, love, and hate,
Envy, anger, are there.
Then, would you quarrels avoid
And peace and love rejoice?
Keep anger not only out of your words –
Keep it out of your voice.

Author unknown

Little Words
"Yes, you did, too!"
"I did not!"
Thus the little quarrel started,
Thus by unkind little words,
Two fond friends were parted.

"I am sorry."
"So am I."
Thus the little quarrel ended,
Thus by loving little words
Two fond hearts were mended.

Benjamin Keech

Spending time together

As part of the general shift that occurs at this stage, we need to learn to be less directive. Another component of the shift is to become friends but in a way unique to the parent-young adult relationship. What does this new friendship look like?

Dan: 'This is one thing I remember my parents saying when I was little. "We're not your friends, we're your parents. Don't treat us like your friends. Don't talk to us like you talk to your friends. Don't disrespect us like you might disrespect your friends." But now I definitely don't look at them as my parents as much as I consider them my friends and room-mates. I have the room up here and they have the room over there. They do their thing, I do mine. I like my parents as people. So when I am home or we spend time together, I really enjoy it.' He went on to define the relationship further: 'I want to backtrack. I don't think my parents are my friends. I don't do with them what I would do with friends necessarily, but we play golf and tennis together and other family things on occasion. I don't go drinking with my parents.'

Fran noted that her relationship with her parents is better now that she's older and lives in a different city. 'I just came back from a visit. I would rather spend time with my parents now than with my friends, especially when I'm so far away. And they are fun now. They like to do things.' One parent noted that he got along best with his children away from the family setting. 'I found if you go out and do something, spending time alone with them, socializing is when we are relaxed and have the best talks.'

Betty shared: 'I had a fabulous experience this year of taking a trip with my daughter and then a trip with my son, who is 22. They were studying abroad so I went over to visit and travel together. It was fantastic. I think it added so much to the relationship. At first I went with my daughter and it was great. Then I was going to go with my son but before I left, I was saying to myself that I didn't know how it would be to travel with him. What are we going to talk about, I wondered? It's going to be so strange. But it was wonderful and we just talked the whole time and I felt like it was a once-in-a-lifetime experience.

'I think you can do that kind of thing if you just say, "Let's go out for dinner" or whatever. I think it makes a big difference until they get married and then your sons... I know I'm making a general statement, but you can't call your son and say, "Would you like to go out to dinner with me?" You can do it with your daughters. I also think having money helps, if it means you can invite your children on a trip or take them someplace special – it really enhances the time together.' Similarly to when the children were younger, we find doing something alone with just one at a time can be an opportunity to encourage closeness.

Along with planned activities, family traditions are a wonderful reason to spend enjoyable time together. Children at all ages look forward to those annual rituals around holidays, birthdays or special days that become cherished events separate from the everyday world. Having a favorite meal, seeing relatives, playing tag football before the big Thanksgiving dinner – these are the memories that bring young adults back home. If we have created meaningful rituals where the family has fun together, they will often plan a vacation or make a cross-country trip to be home and celebrate those special times.

Young adults acknowledged that they enjoy spending time with parents who are both positive and fun. They don't want their parents to try to act younger – like going to bars or taking drugs with their children. They don't want us to be bossy or authoritarian, but they still look to us for guidance. They want a friendship, but with dignity – so the young woman in the previous chapter longed for a dad, not a daddy. She viewed her father as acting like an adolescent, being preoccupied with his own social life, ball games, and so on, rather than being emotionally available as the pillar of strength and support she needed.

Sounds confusing? To some extent, it is – for all of us. We are all trying to find a comfort zone that meets everyone's needs.

Helping young adults to see parents as people

Speaking of everyone's needs, so far we have focused on what our young adults need from us. What about occasions when we wish for a little more attention, sympathy and/or understanding from them? Here are some comments from parents:

Joan: *Let's say one of your kids just happens to call on the day when you're feeling blue or wrestling with something and just feeling down or even tearful. What I do is sort of pull myself together. If they ask, 'How are you?' I say, 'Fine, pretty busy' instead of saying (and I don't do this but maybe it's appropriate), 'You know I feel really awful and I'm really worried about whatever...' That's who I am at that moment, but I don't do that.*

Terri: *You've never done that?*

Joan: *Not much. When they live at home and they are adults, they see tensions. Then I have said, 'Things are a little tense right now,' but they also see you get over it.*

Tad: *So isn't that a double message?*

Joan: *I don't know. Probably.*

Tad: *You say we don't tell them, but they don't ask. We don't tell them and then if we don't get sympathy, we are resentful.*

Terri: *If we say anything personal about us, it seems they're very uncomfortable.*

Dorothy: *But kids don't want to know too much about what's going on with their parents.*

Joan*: I would like our children to know me as a person. I don't think they need to know intimate details of our relationship. I think they just want to know positive things, not unpleasant things.*

Terri: *Well too bad.*

Dorothy: *They also don't know we grew up. Whenever they left us was where they left us.*

Terri: *What do you mean?*

Dorothy: *Well, I grew significantly. I changed. Melissa left home when she was 14 to go to prep school [private school that prepares pupils for college or university]. She's 28 now, so for much of my adult life she didn't see what was happening. I went to graduate school [post-graduate college] after she left home. I'm significantly more mature, more independent and, I hope, a more interesting human being. She has no idea. She thinks I still think the same things that I thought then. When my kids want to reach me in the daytime, they still call me at home. I'm never at home. I'm at work, but they haven't moved me out of the house yet.*

Elise: *Exactly. Tina came home at Christmas and I said exactly that to her. I said people don't stop growing when they've reached 18, 25, or 30. I've probably changed as much between 40 and 55 as she has between 15 and 25. There's a process that goes on all through life. But they hear us thinking what we would have said years ago.*

Dale: *That's that family trance when your kids leave home and they are independent, but when they come back, the old habits return and they see us in the same ways.*

Betty: *I find that my situation is different. I don't know if anyone else is a single parent, but I think that has to do with my situation being different. It changes the relationship because it's not two parents as a unit dealing with children. Maybe it puts you in a weaker position, I don't know, but in that weaker position you end up having a more focused and stronger relationship with your children. I think they see me very much as a person because I have always told them things about myself and changes in things I was* *going through, so I think they're in touch with that. Also I say anything I want and that feels very good. I don't know if it feels good to them. I feel half the time they just laugh at me. Maybe a quarter of the time they don't listen, another quarter of the time it might open up a real discussion and they might say, 'I didn't see it that way' or 'That's a good idea'. I'm not afraid to say anything I want and they're not afraid to not listen to me or tell me I'm wrong, so it doesn't cause problems.*

Joan: *Your kids can't have empathy until they get older. I remember a daughter of mine saying she didn't understand what I went through in motherhood until she had a baby. It takes a long time for them to have empathy with their parents, particularly if you become ill. I think partly that is the fear of their parents disintegrating, maybe just the fear that they don't want to see you age. On the one hand, I think you absolutely have to shift, to allow them a lot of decision-making when they're growing up, otherwise how are they going to learn? At the same time I have the feeling that parents aren't saying to them, 'You know, I don't feel good tonight' or 'I don't have this' or 'I don't have that' – whatever it is. We hold ourselves in trying to be this perfect parent.*

While some parents feel their children don't want to see them as anything but fine – both physically and emotionally – many young adults feel the opposite. Our children always notice when one of us seems upset or preoccupied. To cover that up makes them feel like children, not like young adults. Instead, they appreciate and feel closer to us when we're honest with them. You don't need to disclose personal details, but say for example, 'Yes, your dad has been having a rough time since his dad died, and he has seemed sad.' This acknowledges their perceptions and makes them feel a part of things. Especially as they get older, most young adults want to be there for their parents and it feels good to be a part of their real lives, the happy and the sad, not just the fantasy of these perfect, unreal parents. To keep them at bay with 'No, everything is fine' often makes them feel like they are still 10 years old when, in fact, they are adults themselves.

Not only is it infantilizing, it may also prevent them from being more open. One young woman said she really didn't know her parents as people. They only give her the outline of their lives – such as 'I had lunch with Nancy today' – but never anything more substantial. So she doesn't feel like sharing anything personal with them and, as a result, she feels her parents don't really understand who she is. While we don't want to rely totally on our young adult as our best friend or sole confidant, the sense of closeness is enhanced by some mutually meaningful sharing.

As part of letting our young adults see us more realistically, it is important (and there's ample opportunity) to share more of the difficult information. This can be anything from professional problems to physical illness, to a family history of depression, alcoholism, or sexual abuse. It's a fairly common experience for an adult in his 40s or 50s trying to cope with depression, for example, to uncover memories or information of childhood trauma. It poses a problem at that age in trying to gather additional information from family members who are no longer alive or are too old to be reliable in their recollections. For example, Fran described her experience: 'I think it would be more effective if parents were honest about what they did as teens because when I was younger I didn't know anything about it. I think if they told me the things they did when they were younger, like in high school, I would've been closer and understood why they were so strict with me. Plus there's a history of alcoholism in my family and they were really strict but they didn't tell us that. They warned us about drinking in general terms, but I think if I had known those things earlier, I would've understood more instead of just learning now that Uncle Ted had a problem and we never knew about it. I'm old enough to know now.'

Showing affection

As part of spending time together, we believe physically showing affection helps cement a positive flow of energy and emotion. Touch is one of our primary senses, as important as seeing, hearing and tasting. The earliest communication with our baby is through touch. Our touch and our cradling soothes and reassures the infant. Unfortunately in our society today, as our children grow, touch is discouraged. In many families there's a great deal of love between parent and child and spouses but it is rarely demonstrated by touching. Teenagers complicate the cultural message by pulling away from hugs or kisses, acting as if that behavior is only for babies or sissies. But if we are honest with our feelings, most people enjoy if not crave making skin-to-skin contact in a non-sexual way.

Hopefully fathers can discard their idea of manliness and hug or kiss their grown son in greeting. Dale says, 'I was working with an Italian man and after he came for a few sessions and got more comfortable, he would give me a big hug and a kiss on both cheeks as he was leaving. At first it made me very uncomfortable, but over time I got to really enjoy this ritual. One day he left without hugging me. Next time I asked him, "What happened?" He explained it was nothing personal, he was just upset. I was surprised at how much this expression of caring meant to me.'

Renee says, 'We have always been a hugging family. But I was surprised when Josh, then six foot one inch in high school, felt comfortable giving me a hug and kiss goodbye in front of his friends when going out.' A pat on the back, a kiss on the top of the head, a hug for no reason are sometimes more powerful than a verbal message, 'I love you.' When we feel the love rather than just hear it, it is a deeper kind of knowing.

For discussion:
- What are some activities you and your young adult enjoy together?
- Discuss ways you might improve the relationship. By reading this book, you are already making some changes. Asking yourself for ideas to change automatically starts a conscious (and an unconscious) creative search.

Dan summed up his advice to parents: 'Say no to criticism, yes to optimism.' This chapter addressed different aspects of redefining and nurturing the young adult-parent relationship: creating space and building respect; improving communication; resolving conflicts and issues in an effective and caring way; spending time together; helping young adults see parents as real people; and showing affection. If we are to nurture our relationship, we need to give our children emotional space to explore, discover, learn and make mistakes. As in any strong relationship, utilizing basic communications skills encourages the development of a strong, healthy, vibrant relationship:

- The 'zip your lips' approach – keeping silent after an action has been taken.
- Really listening empathetically, without interrupting or trying to explain our point of view before the person has truly finished.
- Being non-judgmental.
- Sticking to the issue being addressed.
- Avoiding labels and name-calling.
- Expressing faith in our young adult's ability to make decisions and choices.

♥ Young adults want to share their lives with us when we make it pleasant and acceptable to do so. There is room for disagreement and difference in opinion if offered in a non-judgmental, non-patronizing way. And we need to feel free to share parts of our lives so we are not viewed as one-dimensional mom or dad. Certainly we can't expect our young adult or anyone else to be considerate of our needs if we don't express directly what those needs are. This is potentially a wonderful phase in our parenting relationship, where we can share interests and experiences and truly enjoy the person our child has become. It helps so much if we can abandon our investment in shaping them and no longer feel that their choices are our responsibility or a reflection of us. They are evolving in detail, but the core essence is the person we love and enjoy in whatever ways work for each family, each parent-young adult combination.

Chapter 3
Living arrangements – in and out

Wherever our young adult children are living, shifts transpire in our relationship with them. When they leave for college, it changes the household dynamics and forces us to adjust our expectations. If they continue to live with their family after high school, they may feel they are entitled to all the freedom of living on their own. Older young adults who have moved out find themselves returning home for periods of time, often for financial reasons. During this decade of their lives, many choose to move in with their girlfriend or boyfriend, a phenomenon widely accepted by the younger generation but not always comfortable for mom and dad. We will look at these various scenarios through the stories of a number of young people and their parents, in an attempt to understand the needs of each person and find ways to deal with these changes as easily as possible.

Living at home

In increasing numbers, young adults are finding themselves living at home for some time during their 20s. The phenomenon of living at home has long been the norm among lower-income families, where it is expected that children stay with the family unit until they marry, moving out only to begin their own family. Raised with the concept of familial interdependence, these young adults are able to gradually shift to more social freedom while feeling strongly connected to their family of origin. But our society pushes individual rights and independence, so for many while growing up as teenagers their fantasy is to 'get away from home, to be on my own'. We will explore two versions of young adults living with their family. First, a younger group who never leave home. They finish high school and enter straight into the workforce or to a local community college, either for financial reasons or because their grades were not strong enough to get them into a college away from home. Second, young adults who move back into the family home after having some time on their own. This group was labelled by some sociologists in the 1980s as the 'boomerang kids' – adult children living with parents, spurred by rising real estate prices, entry-level salaries that don't match rental increases, college debt and the later age for marriage.

Paul Attewell, a sociologist at the Graduate School of the City University of New York, is studying the grown-up live-at-homes and calls them 'incompletely launched young adults'. He has noted an acceleration in the numbers of live-at-homes, especially in big cities such as Boston, Washington D.C., and New York in the past decade. His research indicates this arrangement is stressful for many parents. He wrote: 'We worry that it is putting off the life transition for parents, and for kids that the situation is unhealthy because they lack the self-esteem that comes from independence.'

Another sociologist at New York University, Kathleen Gerson, disagrees. She feels that parents and offspring in their 20s are closer today than previous generations, so there is less conflict in living together. One mother of eight children calls these live-at-homes 'nesters' and extols the pleasures of having this special time together. Perception is everything.

Janney, the oldest of four, had to come home straight after high school classes ended so she could babysit for her siblings until her mom got home at dinner time. After she graduated and enrolled in a local community college, she was still expected to babysit every day, as well as keep up with a full course schedule and hold a part-time job to earn her own spending money. In addition, she had the same curfew as a college student that she had in high school. She felt her parents were treating her as a much younger teen and resented that she had no time for a social life. She was miserable and had a lot of conflict with her parents until she was able to transfer in her sophomore (second) year to a college in another state.

Jared, the youngest of four and the only child living at home, went straight to work as a computer programmer after high school. As his graduation present, Jared and his dad turned an attic space into an apartment where he would have more space and privacy. Always a reserved, shy person, Jared had a few good friends with whom he mainly listened to music, played computer games or hung out at the diner. His parents, Alice and Ray, had little need to establish formal rules or expectations as Jared had dinner with them most evenings, then went to his room, out with friends or on occasion watched TV with his parents. He was happy to help with lawn work or chores when asked. The agreement was that after he paid off his car debts, he would start paying them a small amount of rent to help with household expenses. Ray was on disability so finances were tight. Alice found it easier to live with Jared once he was out of school. Previously she worried if he had done his homework and handed in his work because he really didn't like being a student. It created a lot of tension between them. Now he was much happier and she found his company enjoyable when he did spend time with them. School is not necessarily the most positive environment for some adolescents and young adults.

Margie and Bill had the opposite happen. While things weren't always smooth, raising Mary had, in general, been a pleasant experience. She had a lot of friends and they enjoyed the youthful energy when kids were in the house or they shared Mary's activities. Mary, 19, had been an average student in high school, getting by with a lot of pushing and supervising from her mom and dad. She went to a college with a program for students with learning disabilities but, even with extra help and counseling, she failed all her courses and had to move back home. Her parents enrolled her at a community college and also expected her to get a part-time job for her spending money. Every night a number of her new friends would come over and stay until late hours in the basement recreation room. Many of these friends were still in high school, only 16 or 17 years old. When her parents found empty liquor bottles and beer cans downstairs, they reviewed the house rules with Mary that there was to be no drinking, and her friends had to be out of the house by 11pm on weeknights and by 1am at weekends. Then Mary got arrested while driving one of these new friends somewhere. John, 17, was carrying an open beer can and some marijuana. He had no penalty as he was a juvenile, but Mary was charged with several counts. At that point Mary's parents felt they had to take a more directive approach. They felt Mary's friends were a bad influence, and she would only get into further difficulty if given too much freedom.

During family counseling sessions with Renee, Margie and Bill initially expressed all their disappointment, anger and frustration to Mary in a very negative way. They berated her and wanted to list everything she had done that showed irresponsibility. Mary sat quietly, unable to defend herself, sinking further and further into the chair. Her already shaky self-esteem was being assaulted and she could only respond with depression and hostility. It was hard for Margie and Bill to stop their tirade and focus instead on a plan. Renee suggested that the family needed to clarify goals and expectations, then establish a series of steps Mary needed to take to reach her goal.

Mary did not want to go back to college at this time. What she wanted was to move out and be independent. Realistically she had run up debts, including a $700 fine from her arrest, and had been fired from her part-time job. She had no concept of money or balancing a checkbook. When asked how much she would need each month to live on her own, she thought a few hundred dollars would do. Mary was shocked when we started to calculate expenses to learn she spent at least $70 to $80 a month on cigarettes alone.

The first step was to establish a gradual plan to enable Mary to become self-sufficient. Like many young adults, she had no concept of what it takes to live month to month. She needed to create a budget, becoming more aware of her monthly expenses, including a payment plan for her debts. She needed a full-time job where she could begin to pay her bills and start putting money aside toward an apartment. Her parents explained she would need the first and last month rent saved plus an emergency fund for unexpected expenses before she could think of moving out on her own.

Instead of battling with Mary and telling her she was too irresponsible to be on her own, Margie and Bill used some problem-solving techniques to look into the future. They let Mary know she could live at home and they would be happy to help her as long she kept her part of the agreement: to respect house rules and to hold a full-time job. While their main concern was that Mary didn't have a direction or marketable skill, they realized she wasn't ready to think long-term.

Many young people take a longer time to mature, to be able to make serious plans and have the self-discipline to work toward those goals. For now it would be sufficient to help Mary become more fiscally responsible. At some future time, either Jared or Mary may decide they need training and/or further education to facilitate career goals. Then they would be motivated to be successful because they had had time to mature, had developed a sense of direction and it was now their choice.

When the young adult has lived on their own for a while, then moves back home, the relationship may be smoother for some families. The parents have had an opportunity to adjust to life as adults, especially if there were no other children living at home, and their grown child has a greater sense of self as separate from their mom and dad. One woman commented, 'I've become friends with my mom as an adult and I see her in a whole different way.' Young adults move back to save money, as rent can be exorbitant just to live in a small, cramped space. Dan, 25, and his younger brother Wes, 20, have returned to their parents' home. They experience the arrangement from different perspectives due to their stages of transition into an adult identity. Dan describes his perception: 'I have a pretty interesting situation because I live at home. My parents don't charge me rent. They don't charge me anything, so I live there and graze in their refrigerator and they feed me. I can't really afford to move out and live the way I want to live, which is why I'm probably still at home. I think they understand that, but on the other hand they definitely don't pay for any of my bills as much as they used to, although they still pay for little things. I pretty much pay for my phone bill, but if I'm going out and I don't feel like going to the bank machine I ask, "Mom, can I have 20 bucks?" and she will give me 20 bucks. That doesn't happen that often. I think they don't have any problems with that. I know a lot of people who are in my same position at work, make basically the same salary and still live at home as well, but I think that some of them pay something like $100 or $200 a month for rent.'

We asked Dan if his parents expected anything in return for not charging him rent. Dan thought for a minute, then replied, 'That's an interesting question. I don't really think they do, but I try to help sometimes. I guess I don't really do that much when I think about it. I help them out when they ask. I don't think they really expect anything of me, although sometimes I feel I want to do things for them – like run errands for them or whatever they ask me to do. However inconvenienced I may be, I almost always say yes because I feel, like, hanging around here, I've got to do something but I certainly don't cook dinner. My mom or dad still gets dinner going when they get home. Do I feel guilty? Not really, because it's just always been that way in my house. I've always lived there except for being away at college or in

California for one year. I came back and now that my brother's back here too, it's just like it has always been. It's just like when we were growing up and a certain part of me thinks that my parents really like that. Sometimes I think they really don't like it but more often than not I think they still kind of like having us around. That's another thing – my parents have a pretty big load to bear with both me and my brother at home – and we're crazy. But they definitely know if they need to crack the whip or really do anything more than ask me where I'm going and when I think I'm coming home, that would be okay with me. They are pretty cool with that, not as cool with my brother though. They have a tighter leash with him. I don't think they really want to interfere in my life and they know I appreciate that.'

Dan's brother has had a harder time returning home as he was just beginning his transition into adulthood. He has balked a lot at his parents' questions about where he's going or when he will be home. When he was at college, they frequently wondered why he wasn't studying and challenged how he spent his free time. After doing poorly, he dropped out of college and worked for a year. Working as a teacher's aide, he found his niche and decided he really wanted to be a teacher. He learned that he has a special rapport with children and a gift for teaching. The job gave him direction and confidence. Now that he's feeling better about himself, he doesn't get so irritated when his parents ask him if he plans to be home for dinner.

Renee commented, 'I think it's hard to make it work because your parents may still want you to say where you're going or to be home early because they don't want to hear you come in at two o'clock in the morning. Or they feel they're giving you a free room and board so you should help them mow the lawn or do errands. It's awkward – you are grown up but you're not grown up. You are still in that little boy setting but you are not a little boy anymore.'

Dan replied, 'Well, I think it has a lot to do with my age group. We are kind of selfish and my parents or parents in general probably don't want to see the selfish kid. They want to see the kid who helps out around the house. You are living there, pick up some slack – be back before five in the morning, you know. You want to say, "Sorry it's not your business when I'm back, leave me alone." Whereas the parents are thinking, "This is my house and you are still part of this household. We tell you when we're going out and when we are going to be home, and we feed the dog when you're not home. You should feed the dog when we're not home." I guess because I'm a little bit older and wiser and more mature, I can see where they're coming from, but my brother still has a hard time dealing with that. He still wants to establish his independence more. I've pretty much resigned myself. Whatever they want.'

Many young adults find it very emotionally difficult to move back home. They view it as a kind of failure or regression, having to turn to their mom and dad after being on their own for a while. Josh was older but had similar feelings to Wes when he moved back to our home. He was 24 when he returned after living in Colorado. While he liked the relaxed lifestyle, he missed being near family and knew that his job there was not what he wanted to be doing long-term. The problem was that he was unclear about what he wanted to do for a meaningful, interesting career. He moved back, a grown man, but feeling like the little boy. To complicate the situation, most of his friends had moved away. He became increasingly depressed, moped around aimlessly and spent a great part of each day sleeping. We have always loved Josh's company. He thinks globally, follows national and world events avidly, and has many interests. In addition to having fascinating discussions, Josh is very funny and entertaining. But during this bleak time, we did not enjoy one another's company. His confusion and depression depressed us. We worried about him and at the same time resented that we would be out of the house working very long hours while he was home doing nothing. We started asking him to help around the house.

In his words: 'I was home and I didn't have a job so it was expected that I would pitch in. Josh is home so let's put him to work. So did I do it? I did, but one, I always resented that I had to do it and two, it's a double-edged sword. Do you have a job? Well, no, I've been painting for four days in a row – how can I look for a job? What do you want from me? I can't do everything. They would leave me notes and things to do. I would get up in the morning and there was a list of things to do for the day. When you are trying to figure out what to do with yourself and how to approach a job search, it's not exactly very helpful to get up and have to paint every day.' Renee commented, 'You did a great job.' Josh laughed: 'I did, the house looked fantastic. It really did.'

Although Josh felt a sense of accomplishment in freshening up the house for us, he also felt a lot of resentment that took a long time to dissipate. He felt obligated to help since we were helping him financially, but it reminded him that he was not acting independently, not doing what he wanted to be doing. When after six months he found a job in New York, we told him he needed to get an apartment of his own. He wouldn't have any time or energy for a social life commuting three to four hours a day if he lived at home. We felt our relationship would improve significantly if we had some distance between us. Although he jokingly reminds us that we threw him out, he would be the first to admit that it was the best thing for him and for our relationship.

The Smiths had a similar situation with Larry. He lived at home for two years, at first unemployed. After he got a job in the city, he commuted for over a year. He had no social life and seemed very unhappy. Following our suggestion, the Smiths told Larry he had to be on his own so he could start to develop friendships and have more in his life than work. They gave him one month to find an apartment in the city or they would do it for him. He found a studio apartment, moved in and soon was going out with friends from work, meeting other young people in the neighborhood and at the gym. Although his parents subsidized his rent for a while, he was much happier being on his own and so they felt better for him. They saw it as a wise, long-term investment to help Larry be more independent.

Dean and Dana were enjoying this new phase in their life. Both their children were married and had started families. They loved the pleasure of spending time with their grandchildren and then going back to the quiet and order of their own home. Plans were underway to redecorate some of the rooms that showed the wear and tear of raising children. Then one day their quiet life was dramatically altered. Karen, their daughter, arrived with her two young children, visibly upset. Her husband had been arrested for embezzling funds from his employer. He had been secretly gambling and suffered heavy losses. He panicked. To cover his debts, he stole money from the company. Her husband was going to prison, their home was being seized, and she and her children had no money. At 29, Karen and her children, aged two and four, moved back in with Dean and Dana, ostensibly just for a few months until she could get her life in order.

Karen decided to divorce her husband but financially she was not well equipped to support herself and her family. She needed to finish college and asked her parents for help. Rather than redecorating, Dean and Dana helped Karen with tuition and watched the children when she was attending classes. The temporary arrangement lasted several years until Karen remarried. There were many arguments during the time together, as is inevitable when three generations share a home. While Karen was extremely grateful for the help, she also resented her parents for parenting her and her children. At times she felt jealous, as her children seemed closer to their grandparents than to her. On her own, she had managed a household and been in charge. Now she felt like the little girl again, with her mom deciding what was for dinner, what her children would wear, when they should sleep.

Since she felt so indebted to them already, she hesitated to ask them to babysit so she could go out at night. Yet she was young, lonely and eager for some kind of social life. For their part, Dean and Dana had offered to help because they didn't want to see Karen and the children out on the streets or on welfare. But they found it difficult to postpone their plans, give up their privacy and time, and feel their home once again taken over by the demands of young, very active children. Karen had originally told them she would take care of everything, but as the months went by, she did less and less to help clean up, make meals, or care for her children. After a particularly bitter argument where hateful things were said, Karen and her parents went for counseling.

The three were encouraged to each state their expectations and needs without worrying about what was right, wrong, okay or mature. Once Dana could express her fatigue and need for help, and Karen could share her feelings of displacement and regression, they were able to establish a plan that met everyone's needs. The family relationships survived those years together, but not without some strain.

When our adult children live with us, whether they are relatively easy to get along with like Jared or Dan, or more challenging like Mary, Wes and Karen, the keys to minimizing stress are:

1 Have realistic expectations and communicate clearly.
2 Avoid screaming matches, name-calling, and hurtful statements. Try to state your needs and wishes in a calm, non-judgmental way.
3 Ask your young adult to help you understand their needs and feelings.
4 Spend some time together enjoying one another's company.

1) In terms of expectations, parents need to clarify – preferably at the beginning of the situation – issues of rent, household responsibilities, hours to keep. These agreements can be modified at any point with discussion among all concerned. Parents can ask their young adult to

keep their area of the house tidy. You need to spell out if you're willing to do things like laundry or food shopping or whether that is entirely up to your son or daughter. Will you share a phone line? If so, how do they want their messages handled? What chores do you expect them to do for the family? Can they come and go or do you need a phone call if they won't be home for dinner or won't be home at all that night? Issues come up as you live together that can be negotiated and refined as circumstances and needs change. It helps to agree at the outset whether any rent will be charged and what will happen if it is not paid. If our goal is to have a positive relationship with our young adult and support their growth, it is important not to let resentment fester unaddressed and to set up the situation to encourage independence and decision-making, rather than dependence and passivity.

2) In addressing conflict, we can find ways to express our needs in a neutral tone of voice that is respectful of our young adult. For example, we might be tempted to angrily say, 'I'm sick and tired of seeing that mess in the bathroom. Why are you such a slob? I'm not your slave, you know.' But that is argumentative, putting our child on the defensive and inviting conflict. Rather we can tell them, 'It really upsets me to have the bathroom be so messy. What kind of plan can we think up to keep it more orderly?' This way we avoid any blaming or name-calling, state our need clearly, and invite the resolution of conflict involving our child in the process. While this approach may take more effort, the pleasant results make it very worthwhile.

3) Sometimes we make assumptions about someone's behavior. Often we are wrong, even when we think we know someone so well. Rather than assume our young adult leaves the bathroom messy become they don't care, we could find time to talk together, asking open-ended questions that require more than a 'yes' or 'no' answer. 'How do you feel things are going for you now?' 'How are you finding it at home?' 'I noticed the bathroom's getting out of hand again.

What's that all about?' You may learn that they are having trouble sleeping at night so they can't get up in time in the morning to get to work or class without rushing out. Or that they are very depressed. Or that they don't feel they should have to clean the bathroom since their brother or sister makes most of the mess and is doing nothing to help. By eliciting information about your young adult's feelings rather than starting with a criticism or attack, there is greater possibility of finding acceptable options.

4) As we discussed in the chapter on friendship, finding pleasurable time together goes a long way toward balancing any difficulties that arise. Dan watches TV some evenings with his parents. He, his father and brother share a passion for golf. Josh likes to go for walks with us and enjoys eating out at his favorite restaurant. Spending time together can be spontaneous and simple, like lingering after a meal for some conversation, cooking together, knocking on the door and asking to listen to the music your son is playing. Even a small amount of pleasant shared time goes a long way toward strengthening the bond with your young adult living at home. It builds up a well of good feelings.

For discussion:
- If your young adult was living at home, what expectations would you have?
- If there has been conflict in the past, how would you like to handle it now?

Living away from home

When our child first moves out, whether to go to college or live in an apartment, it may be their first experience of being truly on their own. For us it may represent a loss, a void in our lives – certainly a shift, especially if it is our last child leaving home. In chapter nine we will address in more depth our needs as individuals going through this phase. But another equally dramatic shift begins to unfold as we redefine our relationship with our child. It may take great effort and a lot of practice but we need to remind ourselves we are not responsible for their lives, for their choices, for their behavior and, most importantly, for their happiness. Our role at this stage becomes one of appreciative audience, consultant and security base.

When our young adult goes away to college, there is a period of adjustment that varies for each individual. We were certain our eldest would have the most difficult time of our three children. When it came time for any new experience, she had a very hard time separating. During her first weeks at preschool, the teachers had to pry her off my body. The first days of kindergarten, she cried when I put her on the bus. When we finally decided she needed the experience of sleep-away camp, we tried to set it up to be a wonderful time. When she was 12 years old she went with her brother, aged 11, to a camp they picked out. She cried in the car all the way to the camp bus and wrote us heart-wrenching letters about how awful camp was. Her brother, in the meantime, loved it. So we dreaded taking her to college. But she met a young man at orientation (a course giving information to university newcomers) and then a cousin's niece within hours of moving in. Both students remained her best friends throughout college. Her transition was remarkably smooth.

We anticipated that Josh would have an easy time. He had always been very independent, plus he had visited his sister at college many times. He knew his way around campus and had become friends with several of Becky's group. And she was at the same college. Much to our surprise, he started to cry in the middle of dinner after we had moved his things into the dorm. After the meal (which he didn't touch), we dropped him off at the dorm and went to our hotel room. An hour later, there was a knock at the door and there he was, looking like the lost boy. His two room-mates were not friendly at all and he had a hard time letting go and settling in.

By the time our youngest was going to college, we were certain she would have the easiest adjustment of all. Always the most flexible, she had learned in infancy to go with the flow. Plus she would be attending the same college where her brother would be completing his studies and she had visited both siblings there over the past four years. Several of her high-school friends were also going to the same college. But for a variety of reasons she had the most difficult adjustment of all, hating it to the extent that she talked initially of coming home and then for the next two years of transferring to another college. She stayed and ended up loving her experience there. She learned a lot from those rough times and so did we.

We learned the importance of the supportive role. There were many tearful phone calls when she told us how hard it was to be in a predominantly sophomore dorm (second-year hall of residence) as a freshman (first-year) where friendships had been formed the year before and she was left out. We heard how her clothes were stolen from the laundry room, how she didn't get invited to join the sorority (female student society) she wanted, and she felt totally overwhelmed by the academic demands. Our instinct was to try to fix it, to give advice, to take over. Instead we listened. We told her we loved her and would support whatever she wanted to do. We stressed our faith in her, reminding her how tough she was in the field hockey games at high school, how determined no matter how big the opponent, how hot and tired she got.

In our book, *Zip Your Lips*, we have a chapter titled 'The You Can Do It Approach'. When our child is experiencing a challenging problem or situation, we remind them of obstacles in the past that they resolved and express confidence that they can handle this new difficulty. Learning to read or tie shoes were once the challenge. Then it was dealing with the bully or friend who turned against you, a parent's illness, or the loss of a grandparent. When we believe in our young adult, they borrow that faith and find some inner resource within themself as well.

When they are in this transition of living independently, they may call for advice on doing laundry or choosing their schedule for the next semester. They may need some guidance with stretching their funds until the end of the month. As a consultant, we can give advice, make suggestions and comments. What we want to avoid is feeling responsible; feeling we have to solve the problem or insure our young adult makes the decision we think is the right one. Often after talking over choices, they may pick Plan B when we thought Plan A was the only sensible way to go. Sometimes Plan B turns out just fine, sometimes it doesn't, but like the butterfly emerging from the cocoon, that is the path our child needs for their development and maturity at this time. Hard as it is – and believe us, it is extremely hard – we need to zip our lips and let them write their own story.

Some parents, whether out of their own need or because of signals from their child, call every day, or visit every weekend if they live nearby. If it is our difficulty in letting go, we need to acknowledge these feelings and try to resolve them while tuning in to our young adult's needs. They may need more space. Or find they get lonelier every time you call, whereas if they didn't hear your voice, they might adjust more quickly.

It's hard not to take over when visiting. Renee remembers, 'I found it so tempting when I visited one of our children and the apartment was dirty (in spite of what they and their room-mates said was a major clean-up before the parents' arrival). I would want to start cleaning and scrubbing or rush out and buy pretty curtains or a new broom – something I thought they should have. Instead I learned to spend the time enjoying their company rather than imposing my needs on them. Of course, they were always interested in going to the grocery and stocking up. But we took our cues from them rather than having our own agenda.'

There are times when more active involvement is appropriate if not necessary. When our child becomes ill or has an eating disorder, we may need to be part of the helping process. Depending on specific circumstances and their age or maturity level, we may start with encouraging them to seek help or we may need to be in touch with professionals. If we are sensitive to the concept of empowering our young adult to take control of their life, we can gauge our involvement and act accordingly.

Whether it is an emergency or just routine life, this is the phase where our role is background; our young adult is foreground, front and center. As much as possible, they are in charge; we are the support system. While it is difficult to relinquish our role of making everything okay, once we learn it, what a relief! We don't have to know the answers; we don't have to fix a problem. We can focus on our own needs and trust our children to take care of themselves.

For discussion:
- Are you having trouble letting go?
- What have you done to support your young adult's independence and growth?
- How would you like to respond in the future?
- In what ways does your son or daughter try to seduce you into taking care of them or taking over altogether?

Moving in with a significant other or cohabiting

In the 1970s, a TV sitcom *Three's Company* had what seemed like a radical premise at the time: two women and one man sharing an apartment. Since we graduated college, dorms have become coed and young people spend a lot of time with friends of both sexes. The *Three's Company* premise today seems more comfortable if two or more friends of mixed gender decide to move in together. What has also become more common are couples who have been dating for a period of time deciding to move in together.

Couples have a variety of reasons behind this decision. For some it is simply the convenience. If both people are living on their own but spending all their spare time together, it seems practical to be in one location paying one rent, one utilities bill instead of two. Others look at it as an adventure, something new to try. For the majority of young adults we have met, their decision is based on the belief that living together gives them an opportunity to really learn what it would be like to spend their lives together. Because they take the commitment of marriage seriously and they don't want to be a future divorce statistic, they are cautious about deciding to marry. While living together is for many not a guaranteed intent to marry, it is viewed as the next natural step in the information-gathering stages leading to a long-term commitment.

Emma found that she learned a lot about herself and about her boyfriend when they were living together. She learned that she can be pretty flexible in many ways, but keeping her place clean and orderly helps her function better. That wasn't as important to Dan so they had to find ways to negotiate an agreement that both could live with comfortably. Fran and Roy had great fun together when they were dating. When Fran's company transferred her to another state, Roy decided to move with her rather than have a long-distance relationship. Fran got important information from this experience. She learned that Roy didn't seem to take the initiative or move fast enough to get a new job. They had major differences about money. Through their discussions, Fran realized she was very insecure and passive in many areas. They decided to go for counseling to work on some areas of conflict.

Mike and Rachel had dated through most of college. After graduation he moved back home with his parents while she got a job and apartment in a town one hour away. They spent weekends together for two years, then he moved in with her full-time. Rachel kept pressing to get married. Mike kept hedging but he really didn't know why until he started living with her. When they were together every day, day after day, he found her too boring and rigid. What was a comfortable, relaxing routine at weekends after a hectic workweek became stifling in sameness on a steady diet. Mike said it was like having a meal. If you had a ritual of going to your favorite Italian restaurant where you got the same meal every Saturday night, you might look forward to it. But if you went every night and had the same dinner, after a while you wouldn't even want to hear that dish mentioned. Rachel wasn't interested in trying new places. She had no hobbies or outside interests. She was content to stay home every night and watch TV. When Mike lived at home, he played in several basketball leagues, had many friends and loved to seek out interesting places to eat, listen to music, hike. These different needs were not so apparent while living apart. The relationship broke off after several months. Mike feels he now has a better idea of what his needs are and what to look for in a potential partner.

Most young adults today are comfortable with the idea of living together, either for themselves or for their friends. Many will continue to live apart until marriage for religious or moral reasons or for a romantic vision. Parents have a wide range of opinions as well, based on similar issues. Eunice lives on the East Coast. She met a young man from the West Coast at college. They continued to date after graduation, managing to see each other approximately every two months as they alternated flying to visit each other. As the relationship continued to deepen, Jack decided to relocate and find a job near Eunice. Her friend asked her if they would move in together. 'Are you crazy?' Eunice exclaimed, 'Remember who my parents are!' Eunice's parents are Korean immigrants with very traditional values. She would never consider living with a man before marriage out of respect for her parents' feelings.

Betty is not comfortable with this option for her children and is struggling with her feelings. 'I'm dealing with this problem right now but it's getting resolved. I'm just letting my children do what they want because they're not listening to me. It's not a moral problem. I think it's more of a social problem because morally I don't think they're doing anything wrong. I have no problem with it, but just socially I was set in my mind – this is what I'm used to. Both my children are in very long-term (more than three years), serious relationships. They both feel they're going to marry the person that they are with and I like their choices very much. The issue came up first when they visited from college. What are the sleeping arrangements going to be? From the beginning, I said they couldn't sleep in the same room. I'd been single for 10 years and I never had anyone stay over because I didn't want them to feel uncomfortable, so they could do the same thing for me because I felt uncomfortable.

'They went along with that but my son and his girlfriend are about to graduate from college and are talking about moving in with each other. I was very upset about that, which is ridiculous. I mean, it really doesn't make any sense but it was my reaction, so I talked to him and his girlfriend and the girl's parents, who want them to get married as I do. The kids think it would be so uncool, saying they're so modern and are a different generation. They are both looking for jobs and feel it's ridiculous to get married at this early age. So I feel I've said everything I could. I gave every argument I could think of.'

Elise has a very different perspective. 'Our daughter is living with the young man that she's been dating for two years. They have been living together for about five months now. I'm thrilled about it. I think it's great. She was raised as an only child and I think she's always only had to think about herself. She has to really accommodate herself to someone else and I think it's a great opportunity for her to become a less selfish person whether or not she ends up marrying him. He is a wonderful person so I feel really good about that. I think in our day and age people who are in love are going to have sex, so what's the difference, why not!'

Another parent commented, 'My father died in 1959 when I was 14 and he had already told us multiple times to live with somebody a year before you get married. This was a very bizarre thing to say back in 1959 to your very young children. Now I don't know if, had he lived to see us into our adulthood and we had done that, he would have felt the same way because my mother was more proper. But I would want my kids to live with someone before they got married and see how it goes. I think there's more to morality than sex. I can imagine a lot of immoral relationships that have nothing to do with sexuality.'

In our discussion groups, parents and young adults talked about the changes between generations in sexual behavior. From curfews and clear-cut standards of behavior, sexually there is now an openness and casualness that many parents find hard to accept. As one parent noted, 'The Pill changed a lot of lives and we sometimes forget that when we talk about the sexual revolution. I mean, that is a big thing. I know that when I was at high school I would have had sex with my boyfriend in a second but I thought, uh oh, I don't want to get pregnant. I didn't know where to get contraceptives. I think that's why our kids don't date more than one person at a time because dating means you are probably sleeping with that person and so there is a different value or standard.'

For discussion:

- What are your views on your young adult living with a boyfriend or girlfriend?
- How would you discuss your opinions together with your young adult without an angry confrontation?

♥ Whether our young adult continues to live at home, lives away, moves back for a while or moves in with a significant other, our goal is to encourage their growth and independence, and maintain a strong, positive relationship. It is not easy to juggle everyone's needs and feelings: the younger young adult wanting to feel more independent; the older young adult who may feel they are regressing by moving back home; the parent who feels their space once again changed. It takes great effort to keep communication open and direct rather than letting resentments fester. When our child lives at home, having clearly defined expectations minimizes opportunities for conflict. A good sense of humor, being able to vent your feelings to your partner or good friend, and getting a break from one another periodically, are all ways to help the parent-young adult relationship stay on an even keel.

As with every generation, there are changes we old folks have to live with. Whether we agree or disagree, like them or not, the changes are here. When our young adult chooses to live with their significant other, we can accept it or, like Betty, express our disapproval or discomfort. Some parents might try to forbid it. Once the couple is together, we can choose to disown our child and sever ties; have contact but be negative, unhappy and create tension; or we can shift our attitude to find ways to enjoy their company and develop a positive relationship. Each choice leads to its own consequence.

Chapter 4

Choice of friends and significant others

As our children are growing up, we try to influence them to follow our values and beliefs. At some point we become aware that our child has opinions and needs that may differ from ours. As our son or daughter becomes a teenager and then a young adult, their choice of friends to date or spend time with can raise issues for us. Since the emphasis in this book is to move from an authoritative position to one of support (from boss to consultant), how do we express our opinions and needs in a positive way? The examples in this chapter offer a range of options as we endeavor to put the greater well-being of our parent-young adult relationship ahead of our need to direct, protect, avoid embarrassment, or be right.

When older teenagers live at home

Once teens turn 18, they believe something magical happens. They are now adult, no longer under their parents' domain. Some 18-year-olds are fairly mature and their parents are comfortable giving them a great deal of freedom. The parents like their friends and trust their judgment in social situations. With young adults like Mary, whom we met in chapter three, and Deirdre, whom we will discuss in chapter five, the trust level is much lower. Mary lives at home after flunking out of college. One source of conflict was her choice of friends. They came over every night, stayed too late, and left a trail of empty beer cans and liquor bottles. After Mary got stopped by police while driving a friend who was holding an open beer can and marijuana, her parents felt they had to set some rules regarding her social life.

Margie and Bill realized they could not forbid Mary to see the friends of her choice. Instead they expressed concern that these new friends did not seem to have any purpose in life other than to party and get drunk. They told Mary that they understood her need to have a social life and to make new friends since many of her group from high school had gone away to college. Margie and Bill set some parameters for socializing in their home, including periodic visits to the family room to enforce the non-drinking policy. Finally they told Mary that she was a very special person, fun, funny, attractive, loyal and considerate. Since she brought so much to a friendship, she needed to take her time and meet the kind of people who would value her and treat her well, not get her into trouble.

It is a very delicate balance between expressing your opinion and criticizing your child. They may feel that criticism of their choices is really a way of criticizing them, their likes, values and personality. So it is extremely important to express our opinion in a positive context. It can be viewed as throwing out another way of evaluating a person, something for your young adult to think about. With a younger daughter or son living at home, there may be greater opportunities to know their friends and to set some limits on contact within your home.

Your young adult's choice of relationship

When asked in a discussion group whether they have had any conflicts with parents about the person they were dating, Janice and Gloria described their parents' disapproval:

Janice: *I knew my dad didn't like a guy I was dating. He was extremely understanding and he said 'You are growing up and you have to make your own decision. I can't choose whom you are going to marry or whom you are going to be with.' I knew he didn't* *like my boyfriend, but he let me figure my way out of it.*

Dale: *So that was a helpful response.*

Gloria: *My parents think my boyfriend could treat me better. Not just as far as being romantic and stuff like that. I agree on some level but not to the extent that they do. My mom thinks I could be better taken care of but it's never been a conflict. I wouldn't stop dating him just because they think it's wrong. I'm going with my own heart.*

Dale: *If a parent says something like that, doesn't it have some influence on how you look at the situation? You hear that message at some level.*

Gloria: *Yes, and I mean it does make me wonder, could I be treated better? I could harbor resentment on some level with him because it's been said to me. And I wouldn't know any different in terms of comparison, so yes, it makes you think when somebody else has an opinion.*

Parents' concerns may range from a general feeling of unease to specific complaints based on the behavior of the person their son or daughter is dating. In some cases, concerns are motivated by religious or ethnic reasons. Debbie's mom objected to her choice because he was Italian: 'My mom has very bad stereotypes of her own nationality, which kills me because she's Italian, which makes me half Italian and I like Italian guys. So I found a guy a year ago and she just gives her opinion of the stereotypes – "Oh, they're all like this, they're all like that, don't get involved." Thanks mom, but I'm with the person and now it's at the point where I don't share things with her about the guy I'm dating. I don't share anything. She doesn't give me that openness to conversation. "How's everything?" "How's he doing?" It's just a very closed relationship with regard to guys.'

Debbie's mother has locked herself into a position that alienates her daughter and cuts off communication. She might have concerns about Italian men, which she could share with Debbie but still invite her boyfriend to the house and get to know him. By expressing an opinion but leaving the door open, she would get information about how the relationship is progressing.

Fran has been dating Roy for two years. While they talk about getting married eventually, Fran has a few reservations. It has been very helpful to be able to express her opinions and worries without her parents turning against Roy. Basically they have taken a neutral approach, serving more as a sounding board than advisers. They validated Fran's concerns as legitimate and encouraged her to take more time before deciding on marriage. But they wisely avoided jumping on the negative bandwagon, knowing there was a good chance Roy might become their son-in-law and they did not want to create bad feelings or put Fran in a position of choosing sides.

Noelle wasn't so lucky. Her mother has always been very critical of her. Mrs M has told Noelle for years that she is a slut, stupid and immature. Because of all the conflict at home, Noelle had been looking for an opportunity to move out. At 23, she worked full-time and had been saving her money. She had been dating a young man, aged 28, for five months. They had started to talk about marriage and were looking at rings. When he asked her to move in with him, her mother told her the young man was only using her and he was unwelcome in their home. Further, if Noelle did move in with him, the family would consider her dead and she would never be able to come to any family or holiday gatherings. This attitude seems even more irrational since Noelle's older brother lived with his girlfriend prior to their marriage for several years with no objection from the parents. Mrs M added further insult, 'If I had known 24 years ago what I know now, I would never have had you.' Mrs M's comments go way beyond expressing an opinion. Her words are hurtful and destructive to the relationship.

Our reservations may be based on the belief that no one is good enough for our precious offspring. We may have preconceived ideas of the person our child should marry. It is easy to assess a potential partner, focusing only on the perceived negatives and overlooking the strengths of a relationship. Many of us judge our young adult for being immature, based on the expectations of a 45-year-old instead of remembering how we might have been at that same age. It is also a danger to look at them as a finished product instead of a work in progress. Dale notes, 'We have both certainly changed a great deal from the people we were in our 20s. Our parents disapproved of some of our decisions in the early years of our marriage.' While it is tempting to criticize our child's boyfriend or girlfriend for not having more direction, or being insecure, too quiet or too uncomfortable in the family setting, we can allow room for maturation and growth. We have to be realistic and not expect perfection. We can focus instead on the qualities that are helpful in balancing our child's personality, common interests the couple shares, the fun they have together. Not all dating relationships end up in marriage so we can be friendly but impartial observers for a while, neither sanctioning nor condoning the relationship. We can take a 'wait and see' attitude, which in turn may help our young adult take time to let the relationship develop at its own rhythm.

For discussion:
- How would you handle it if your son or daughter seemed to be getting seriously involved with someone you didn't like?

Sleeping arrangements

At some point in the dating relationship, we may sense or become aware that our young adult is sexually involved. Since attitudes now are so different for many of us than the society in which we were raised, each parent will have to decide their own beliefs regarding a couple sleeping together in their home. One parent tells her children that they are not going to sleep with their significant other when they come home to visit. 'I say in my house, you don't do it. What you do on the college campus is your choice – I'm not there. I'm not a policeman but in this house you are not going to sleep together.' When her daughter questioned her, commenting that she had been going out with her boyfriend for three years and that it was a very serious relationship, she had no response. Another parent suggested that these are different times and said, 'I think you have to respond. It depends on the situation.'

Terri commented, 'I'm having trouble with the generations. I think we're talking about the differences because there is a generational shift. When we were dating, would we ever have dared to bring a date home and sleep in the same room with them? We'd never have even dared to ask our parents, would we? It's not right or wrong – it's a tremendous generation shift.'

Dan has been seeing Kara for five years. When they were at college, his mother was adamant. 'My mom said throughout high school and college, "There's no way a girl is going to come over here and sleep in your bed with you, just no way. It won't happen." "Why mom?" I'd ask. "Just because it's not right," she'd say, or "I just don't want it to happen. I don't want other people knowing that their daughter has slept in my son's bed with him." I was like, all right, it was just that she thought that way and I respected her wishes. Then I guess it changed when we came back from California. I don't know, because then it was all right.' Dan's mom felt it was not appropriate for high school- and college-aged students to sleep together in her home. When Dan was in his mid-20s and had lived with his girlfriend in California for a year, she seemed more comfortable with the idea.

Rachel's family has a different policy. She stressed her parents' attitude is not personal, but based on firm convictions. 'In my family that would never happen in a million years, even though my parents are very liberal. My sister was engaged for a while and her fiancé did not even sleep in our house. He lived in the same town so when they both came home from college or later to visit, it was always awkward. At five in the morning he would go home, which sounds crazy since they were getting married. Even now, if I brought somebody home, I wouldn't even attempt it. We might sneak around, but my parents would disapprove. I mean, that would never happen. If I did, if they knew about it, they wouldn't say anything but they might make a crack about it indirectly. But we respect that that's not going to happen in our house. I have very liberal parents so it's like a contrast with them. I don't really know why.'

Honest, direct discussion is the best way to handle the situation, preferably before it comes up. If John is bringing his girlfriend home for Christmas and it is the first time they are visiting together, you can let John know that his guest will be sleeping in with his sister if you wish them to have separate rooms. By stating the plan in advance, a couple will have realistic expectations for the arrangements. If you are comfortable allowing them to be together, you may want to ask them about their comfort level – should you get one or two rooms ready? While we have no control over our young adult's behavior while they are away from home, we can maintain our beliefs and codes of behavior in our own home. Usually our children have us pretty well figured out, but there may be some testing and, as in all aspects of the relationship, ideas discussed in a direct, non-judgmental way minimize the opportunity for future misunderstandings and bad feelings.

For discussion:

- Has this issue come up in your household?
- Do you and your partner agree about the family policy? If not, think

of options to present your opinions to your young adult.

- How would you open the discussion together?

When marriage is proposed

First we worry that our baby will be born healthy with all its fingers, toes and parts in place. As our child develops, we worry that we are up to the task of raising a happy, self-confident and independent person. Once our child grows up, a common parental concern is whether they will find a mate who makes them happy and who fits into the family. Many issues become stirred up when our child becomes seriously involved in a romantic relationship. How can we be supportive if we truly doubt the choice of a future mate? How can we help our child discuss their own feelings and concerns in a way that won't be held against us, should they indeed marry that person? There is perhaps no other area where we seem to feel so confident that we know what is best for our child. We see the potential for being hurt in the choice of an insincere or inappropriate friend (our opinion) and want so much to protect our child. Or we take a liking to a potential partner and, wanting that person in the family, try to force a relationship when it may be on shaky ground. Or the opposite occurs. We have known parents who went to dire lengths to alienate their child's significant other, believing in their hearts that they alone knew who was the best choice for their son or daughter.

Sometimes the choice of a partner is a natural fit and the family welcomes this new addition with open arms. That is the ideal beginning to the fairy-tale ending and they live happily ever after. There are some stories where the family seems to like the future member more than their own child does. Walter related, 'I ended up getting engaged because my parents really liked the person I was with. We were together five years and first my grandma then my mom started asking, "When are you getting married?" When I went to Florida with my family on vacation, we went into a jewelry store just looking at things. My mom came out with a ring and sort of suckered my fiancée into trying things on, trying to get an idea what she liked. Later mom said, "This is what you want, right?" and I said I guess so, and it just sort of happened. We're separated now. I'm single and it's the greatest thing in the world, but what an unbelievable conflict because it was like I was doing something they wanted and they were pushing me. Later my mom came to apologize and said, "I'm sorry if you think I pressured you but I thought I was just going with the plan." I don't know if they thought that's what I wanted or that's what I should have done, so maybe they thought they would just give me a little nudge.'

We can be friendly and welcoming without rushing our young adult into any situation. It is important to take our cues from our child. One mother of sons loved the young woman her eldest son was dating. She was anticipating that time when she would have a daughter-in-law to go for lunch with or just have time to talk together. After her son and his girlfriend had been going out together for several years, she mentioned to her son that she would be happy to accompany him to Uncle Sam's, who happened to be a jeweler. She was somewhat taken aback when her son angrily replied that they weren't ready to think about marriage yet and not to mention the subject again. Relatives can be so nosy! Dale remembers, 'I kept asking my nephew every time I saw him if he had a girlfriend yet. I was just making conversation but he found it pretty annoying. Finally, at some family gathering, after I asked my usual question, he replied, "Uncle Dale, when I get a girlfriend, I promise you'll be the first to know, but don't keep asking me." I kept my part of the bargain and, sure enough, several months later he informed me that he was dating Courtney.'

What if we have serious doubts about our child's choice of a future mate? How can we be honest, yet helpful and supportive? Kate divorced her husband after 20 years of an abusive marriage. While it took her a long time to find the courage to seek a divorce, she felt hopeful that family life without constant tension and violent outbursts would be helpful to her children. Shortly after the separation, her daughter dropped out of college and moved in with her boyfriend. They announced their engagement and started to plan a wedding. Kate watched with dismay as familiar patterns started to emerge. Susan would stop over to visit and be red-eyed from crying. When Kate questioned her, she would play down the fact that she and her fiancé had been arguing. Once when the family was invited to Susan's and Jim's apartment for dinner, the couple started bickering and Jim threw a plate against the wall. They all watched it smash into pieces. The rest of dinner everyone ate in silence. Kate and her children left shortly after the meal was over.

At first, Kate assumed Susan would see that she was repeating the pattern of abuse with which she grew up. When Susan continued to minimize the problems while firming up wedding plans, Kate decided she had to express her concerns. Kate was cautious in choosing her words, knowing that in spite of her objections, Jim might be her future son-in-law. She reminded Susan of some of the problems in her own marriage, which Susan had witnessed growing up. Kate shared what she had learned about the patterns of abuse, the fact that it is cyclical – an outbreak followed by a honeymoon period of peace and promises. She explained that the origins come from insecurities and the need to control, as well as the likely history of that person's own abuse in childhood. The abusive behavior is not caused by excessive drinking but may be exacerbated by it. Then she expressed what she had observed in Jim's behavior that fit these patterns. She encouraged Susan to go for counseling and think about returning to college.

Susan continued to deny any problems. The marriage went ahead on schedule. Several years later, Susan moved back home with her family and sought a divorce on the grounds of mental cruelty and alcoholism. Kate saw the problems but there was little she could do to forestall the marriage and subsequent hurt for her daughter. She couldn't refuse to pay for the wedding since the young couple were paying for it themselves. To refuse to attend might have only created more tension and left Susan without a supportive base to rely on when she was ready to seek help.

Even when we see our child being hurt in a relationship and want to offer advice and protection, we can do little more than express our concerns and support in a positive way. We don't want to humiliate our child or cut off the relationship. Humiliating our child, making threats, or cutting off the relationship rarely changes their decision. It only creates more problems in its wake and leaves them without a supportive network that only a parent offers.

There are occasions where parents feel strongly that they cannot accept their young adult's choice. Tom, aged 26 and Catholic, started dating Barbara, aged 25 and Jewish. After a year of dating, they decided to move in together and after another year, announced their engagement. Tom's parents were very unhappy about the relationship. They used every phone conversation to criticize Tom and say what a disappointment he was to them. Barbara's parents went even further. They refused to have any contact with her, either by phone, letter or directly as long as she stayed in a relationship with someone of a different religion. They didn't allow themselves the opportunity to get to know Tom or to watch the young couple together so they couldn't know that in so many ways they were very well suited to one another.

Renee recalls, 'Something similar happened in my own background. When my father, at 30, told his Orthodox Jewish parents that he intended to marry my 26-year-old mother – who was Methodist but studying to convert to Judaism – my grandfather forbade him to marry her. Once they were married, gradually and with time the family came to love my mother. When we visited them, everyone welcomed us – including my grandfather, who talked with my mother and the children, but he never again spoke to my father for disobeying his orders. When we got engaged and Dale told his parents about my background, his mother asked him not to marry me because by Orthodox standards I was not Jewish. For my mother and me, the religious differences created dissension and tension in family relationships for many years. It eventually worked out for me with my in-laws. I don't think my mother ever got over these initial scars of being rejected.'

When our eldest daughter seemed to be getting very interested in someone not Jewish, Renee wrote a letter and sent it to each of our children explaining her hope that they would marry someone of the same religion. She shared in more detail her own family history mentioned above. She stressed that marriage between any two people is hard enough. It helps to have similar backgrounds and the shared rituals of religion. She still believes this to be true, but as the relationship developed and our daughter was obviously committed to a future with Bill, our attitude shifted to getting to know all the wonderful qualities that she saw in him and to help him feel accepted and welcome in our family. It sent a really important message to our daughter that we cannot make her choices for her, but we will respect her decision. Rebecca has since told us many times that it means so much to have the love and support of her family when she does make important choices.

It is human nature to feel comfortable with people who are similar, and to feel ill at ease with someone of another religion, race or culture. And there is a certain chauvinism in wanting your own culture to continue. Hispanics, blacks, whites, Asians, Catholics, Jews – we would all probably prefer our children to find a mate within our own community. These communities no longer have such defined boundaries and the world is shrinking. There are more interfaith and interracial marriages than ever before. If we have raised our children to be independent, conscientious, self-aware and tolerant of others, we need to trust our offspring in their choices, whether it is a career, lifestyle or partner. Even if we believe the choice is a poor one, we can remember that life is a series of lessons and challenges. Often we grow the most out of difficult situations.

For discussion:
- Do you know of any families torn apart by the child's choice of a partner?
- How would you deal with it if your son or daughter wanted to marry a person you didn't like?

When your young adult is homosexual

Many teenagers become aware of sexual attraction to their own gender during high school. In an effort to fit in or to try to be heterosexual, they may actually date the opposite sex or deny their true feelings. However, as they begin to experience the world outside the limits of high school, they may be more open about their homosexuality. Parents may have their suspicions or may not sense it all, but as young adults become more secure in their sense of self, they may come out of the closet.

Most parents find it difficult to deal with the feelings this statement of identity stirs up. Often an initial reaction is one of self-blame. For too long, society's response to homosexuality was to blame parents, as if to say an overbearing mother or a passive, distant father could cause a child to become homosexual. Parents may start examining child-rearing behaviors to search for lapses or wrongdoing. To complicate the situation, some religions teach that homosexuality is a sin. These feelings of guilt and/or shame are a heavy burden to bear, for the young adult and the parents.

In recent years our culture has been more open and accepting of the gay community, with television shows like *Ellen* and *Mad About You* as well as famous stars talking about their sexual preferences. Still, as a whole, society is not very accepting of this lifestyle, which places a further burden of secrecy on employees in their work situations and, for some, within their extended families. Parents with a lesbian daughter may feel embarrassed or uncomfortable telling relatives that their daughter is living with another woman. And parents may have to deal with the knowledge that they might not have grandchildren from that union, although there are exceptions.

One family dealt with the knowledge that their daughter was lesbian by getting to know her significant other and including her in the immediate family gatherings. However, they were too uncomfortable to tell extended family directly. When family gatherings like a wedding or grandma's 80th birthday occurred, their daughter was bringing her 'room-mate'. The women were expected to act like friends, not lovers, in front of relatives. Clare found this very uncomfortable but easier to live with than the idea of hurting her very conservative parents. Clare's mom worried that the lifestyle was too unstable, that Clare would never know the strength, security and love of a long-term relationship like she had had with Clare's father.

For many years, Clare answered her parents' suspicions with lies, sensing their disapproval and fearing their rejection if she told them the truth. It was only after graduating college and living on her own that she felt secure enough to talk with them about her lesbianism. Clare and her parents are still evolving in their ability to deal with her girlfriends and search for a committed relationship. It has been a tremendous comfort to Clare to maintain her close relationship with her parents, even while knowing this is not the path they would have chosen for her.

Leigh has a lesbian daughter, Kathy, who is in a long-term committed relationship. She and her husband like Kathy's mate very much. Kathy has had two in vitro pregnancies. Together, she and her partner are raising their family and, according to Leigh, doing a wonderful job. Leigh's ex-husband, Kathy's father, could not accept her lifestyle and has refused to see her or his grandchildren for more than 10 years.

Donald first told his parents he was gay when he was 20 years old. At 22 he fell in love and moved in with Arthur. During their years together, both men were very close to one another's families, sharing holidays, Sunday dinners and family gatherings. When they broke up after seven years together, Donald relied on his family to help him deal with the loss. He noted that their support and love were key factors in helping him resolve his grief.

❤ The choice of our young adult's friends or partners does not reflect our own needs, wishes, or value system. When we equate their choices with our identity, we may feel a sense of rejection, guilt and sadness. But we have raised our children to find their own way in the world and the fact is, no matter how old our children get, love and approval from mom and dad is – and always will be – one of their highest needs, offering them a strong sense of security and enhancing their self-worth. If we can put our own egos aside and be open to our children's choice, we increase opportunities for joy and closeness, through happy times as well as challenging experiences from which we learn so much.

Chapter 5

Supportive ways to deal with financial issues

As we explore the various kinds of financial issues and ensuing questions that arise for parents and offspring, it is crucial to stress that we are looking at options, not rules or formulas. The ways in which parents choose to offer financial support may vary widely, depending on the parents' economic situation, value system, philosophy of child rearing, the young adult's situation and many other factors. This chapter is not suggesting any 'right' ways as we examine these variables. However, as we do throughout the book, we are emphasizing the 'how you do it' part of the picture.

Since our goal is to shift to a more positive relationship with our child, our communication in this area needs to be phrased in supportive ways. As each family decides how to handle the numerous issues about money, we can open discussion and express our opinions with the intent to 1) clarify our expectations, goals and decisions and 2) empower our son or daughter to make decisions and take responsibility. If our intent is either to take control or be critical of them, no matter what our action may be, the interaction will most likely not go well. Before we discuss any issue with our child, it is always helpful to do a personal check-in and acknowledge our intent. Sometimes it is hard to acknowledge that we want more control or feel a need to manipulate a choice to our way of thinking. Any money given with a hidden agenda has the potential to cause major damage in a relationship.

Some families find it uncomfortable to discuss financial issues. Decisions are made or money is given with little or no discussion. What we have learned in dealing with our grown children is to be thorough and clear in discussing our financial interactions. In hindsight, we regret we didn't always spell out how much was being given, for what purpose, and the expectations involved. Sometimes less is more, but in financial matters the more discussion and clarity between parents and young adults, the less room for resentment and disappointment down the road.

As in any discussion, we need to state our position in positive terms. There will be numerous examples in the chapter but the essence is to choose our words carefully. It is just as easy to say, 'We have some concerns that your bills aren't getting paid and would like to make a plan with you' as to say in a demeaning way 'You are so irresponsible and careless with money. You never had any sense of money. What a mess you've got into.' We have had sessions in our practice where an angry parent went on and on, repeating too many times a litany of complaints wildly while their child either got angrier and more defensive or shrank further into the chair. In the 'zip your lips' approach, you state your concern or position once and then wait for a response. We want to invite participation and feedback from our son or daughter, which is empowering. We don't want to infantilize or diminish them by name-calling, generalizations (like 'You never...' or 'You always...'), or by taking over the process.

Families that cannot afford to offer financial aid

For some families, there is no decision to make. There simply is no money available to help older children. For these young adults, the expectation is clear. After high school or college, you are on your own. Debbie expresses her experience of being on her own: 'My parents don't have money, which means I don't have money. I mean, I have money – I survive at college by working, getting a minimum wage. It helps to pay the phone bill every month and that dreaded Visa bill that I have come to know. Without that Visa, I don't think I could have survived college so far. I'm keeping up with it. I don't ask for money because I know there is none – and I've given up asking for help. I think in a sense I was forced into independence before many of my friends. Everything is dependent on me. I have to be responsible for my books, clothes, food and spending money. My parents aren't helping me so money is a very big issue. There's not one day that goes by that I'm not scared about money, wondering if I can afford this or that. If my friends are going out, I can't because I don't have the money. So it's hard, but I've learned to deal with it better over the years.'

As a parent with limited means, Betty has a different perspective: 'In my situation, I just didn't have money to give my kids and even in college, believe it or not, I'm not giving them money. As a consequence of that, they are very interested in making money and getting high-paid jobs – they're very focused in that direction. I don't know if that's a good thing, either, because that's more like one or two generations ago, but that's something they really think about and try to figure out how they're going to do it.'

These young adults have little ambiguity about money or responsibility when they have no choice but to be self-sufficient. While it might be very difficult at times, there is a tremendous feeling of pride in each success. Some of the past century's most successful entrepreneurs started life in impoverished conditions and used their determination to guide them into positions of wealth and power. Indeed, in previous generations, particularly in immigrant and poor families, children were expected to earn money to contribute to the family's survival. Atlanta Hawks basketball star Dikembe Mutombo sends his paycheck to his tribal family in Africa. As with all realities, when a young adult is self-supporting, there is a positive side and a downside. Parents can also be extremely helpful giving advice and evaluating options – for example, with loans. Money isn't the only way to help.

Now that we have blurred the line between childhood and adulthood, it is harder to determine when help is warranted and when independence is to be expected. Even for families with limited means, the cultural value to give our children a better life often guides our financial decisions. Kate divorced an abusive husband when her children were 11, 15 and 20. She is an LPN (Licensed Practical Nurse – a nurse who has completed a training course of a lower standard than a registered nurse) who has only been able to find part-time hospital work with no benefits. Because of a very poor divorce settlement, her ex-husband pays very little child support and has refused to pay his share of extra expenses such as orthodontic work, books for college, and a new outfit for confirmation. She struggles every month just to pay her bills. The small savings she had when the family home was sold have dwindled to almost nothing and she has no retirement account.

In spite of knowing how tight finances are, all three children make demands on her and get angry when she refuses. Her eldest child has a responsible job but overspends and constantly looks to her mother to bail her out. The middle child, now in college, has not held any part-time job for longer than a month and expects his mother to give him spending money. They all play on her guilt for breaking up the family, depriving them of a more affluent lifestyle. Kate needs to learn to set clear boundaries and expectations, and then, most importantly, follow them through. By telling her children, 'This is what you are expected to pay for, this is what I can give', she will decrease the amount of turmoil and hostility in the family and encourage each child to take responsibility for their own needs.

For discussion:
- When you cannot or choose not to give your young adult money, what words do you use to clarify your behavior and needs?
- In what other ways do you demonstrate support for your son or daughter?

Full financial support

When parents have the capability, it is understood that they will support their son or daughter through college. Some parents make a contract in the beginning, saying clearly, 'We will pay for four years of college, then you are on your own.' A fifth year of college (which has become more common) or graduate school (which has become more of a necessity in many occupations) is negotiable. During this period of financial dependence, some parents work out a budget so that their child knows exactly how much they have to spend each month. Some families ask them to work during the summer, breaks, or even part-time at college to furnish their own spending money. Other parents arrange credit cards and money to be available with no limits or clarification.

In our opinion, the more responsibilities are spelled out, the more comfortable everyone will be in the long run. It helps the young adult to know just what funds are available and who pays for major purchases such as a new winter coat, shoes or a computer. When the Visa or phone bill gets sent home to mom and dad, there is room for criticism and anger when the bill is too high or parents don't approve of the way monies were spent. If young adults have a budget and checking account, it can be educational and empowering to have bills directly sent to them to be paid within the budgeted funds. Even with a carefully detailed plan, unexpected expenses occur that require negotiation for who will pay. If, for example, a young adult budgeting their monthly allotment has a car that suddenly needs a new transmission, parents may opt to pay because the car is necessary to get to and from college and a job; they may offer to lend the money or they may leave it up to their child to find the funds. Each scenario may be appropriate to that family's situation.

For discussion:
- Have you conveyed the philosophy underlying your financial agreement?

- Have you clearly spelled out what this financial support is intended to cover and what items, if any, you are willing to pay for?
- Are you helping too much?
- Do you zip your lips about your young adult's choices? (This may be the hardest question of all.)

When and how to supplement income

There are a wide variety of attitudes and situations when it comes to supplementing the income of our young adult. One father in a discussion believes in helping his children. Lionel explains: 'I feel money is like love. If you've got it, what else is it good for? If you can't use it for your own kid, what are you saving it for? What are you going to wait for? Sure, you want to have a nest egg for when you retire to take care of yourself comfortably, but my feeling is, if it's there and they ask for it, it's available. It depends on what you're talking about too. If your son or daughter says, "I don't feel like working now, I just feel like...give me the money", it might be different. But it's not easy to buy a house today even if you have two responsible members of society. So if your child is married and they want to buy a house but they just can't get a down payment together, if it's really that important, why not help?'

Lionel loves his children and can afford to help them. He views it as his pleasure to share his good fortune with his grown children. Edward has the opposite situation. His father is a very successful builder. Edward left his father's business to start his own company in another state when he married. He has struggled to build up his business, needing financial assistance several times in the past seven years. Each time, he approached his father for a loan, making it clear he would rather repay a relative than the bank. Each time, his father refused. Although Edward was able to secure the loan and is building his own successful business, he interprets his father's refusal as a lack of love, especially when his parents have taken his sister and her family on trips to the Caribbean. More about perceived inequalities later in the chapter, but many young adults interpret lack of financial support (when the parent has the means) as a sign that they are unloved and unworthy.

Jonathan was taking a very rigorous university course in chemical engineering. He asked his parents to buy him a new computer, which would be very helpful in his studies. They told him they couldn't afford it. A short time later, his parents bought an antique dining table with chairs and boasted to the family about the bargain they got. It is hard not to view these parents' priorities as selfish or unloving. When, for some reason, a parent decides not to help and the money itself is not the issue, it might be helpful to explain your rationale to your son or daughter. By saying something to the effect of, 'We love you very much and we understand you would like some help, but we choose not to help you at this time, and here is our thinking...', you can separate the issue of love from the other factors more easily.

Another parent in a discussion group did not feel she would help her children financially beyond paying for their education. As she sees it, 'I feel very strongly that I have treated my kids to a very nice lifestyle and it's important that they work in the summers and through college. At the end of all this education, they should be able to support themselves in the style to which they have become accustomed. And if it's not the style to which they have become accustomed, they'd better become accustomed to a new style because I'm not always going to be there to support them in a way that they may not be able to do on their own. I believe you have to learn to live within your means. I feel very strongly about that and I think if you don't have the means – for example, if you choose to be an artist because that's what you want to be – I think that's great. Whatever my kids want to do is okay with me. Let's take the example of being a graduate student who doesn't make a lot of money, then you have to learn to live in that lifestyle.

'I see too many people who aren't happy with what they have, always wanting more. Everything in life is choice and if you start out and you're not making that much, well, that's what you live on. That's what I did. I didn't have anything in the beginning and always stressed to my kids that happiness should not depend on having material things. So you don't have fancy clothes and designer labels, you don't live in a fancy place – you have to walk. Then you have to adapt to that lifestyle and do that for a few years. You can work really hard or you can live like that for many years, and that's it. That's reality. I'm very big on reality, because that's what it is. Perhaps it's harder for our children because they have got used to great lives and they might not have that level of comfort in the future, and I've talked with them about it.'

When money is given to subsidize a young adult, it may be manipulation on the parents' part or may at least feel like it is from the young adult's perspective. In the parents' discussion groups, various scenarios were raised to suggest that we are more likely to give money when we approve of our child's plan. If they need money to go to graduate school for a profession that is marketable, such as law or accounting, we are more likely to support that than a degree in ancient musical instruments. If they move to a big city because of a job offer with great potential but low starting salary, we might offer to help with additional expenses. If they decide to move to the city for 'an adventure' and can only find a job waiting tables, we may be less generous.

Often parental decisions of financial support seem to depend on whether or not they approve of their young adult's choices – whether a life partner, job or a new home. How many parents have told their child that they will not pay for a wedding if they choose someone of a different religion or if we simply do not approve of the potential partner? As one parent said, 'I think, honestly, this is reality. If your child marries someone you think is just fabulous and wonderful, and they love each other, and they're the right religion and the right everything – you can't help but feel more positive about wanting to help that relationship, more than you do in a relationship where you are not so happy with their choice.'

Another parent found himself criticized by his son who complained, 'You only give me money to do what you think I should do. That's not fair.' He answered his son by agreeing that it is unfair but life itself is not fair. It's a democratic principle in a way; support what you like, don't support what you don't like. Is that being authoritarian? Or is that supportive? One young man answered that it looks like it is supportive but it is also controlling and manipulative.

Fran comes from a state with an excellent educational system. She did her undergraduate work in her home state and received the benefits of lower tuition. When it came time for graduate school she wanted to study and live in New York City. Her parents wanted her to stay nearby so they offered to pay all in-state tuition and expenses. To sweeten the deal, they offered to buy her a condominium. She chose to move to New York. She obtained student loans and took several part-time jobs to support herself. While she loves living in New York, she sometimes thinks she acted foolishly, as life would be so much easier had she stayed in her home state.

Parents may want to help their young adults financially as it gives them pleasure to do so. This may be especially true if the parent had to struggle in their early adult years. Now with their own financial comfort established, they are pleased to make life easier for their children. Another motivation expressed by some parents is their children's safety. A parent might prefer to subsidize the rent for a daughter to find living arrangements in a safer area. Many parents help finance a better car when the current model is not safe to drive. They may choose to pay for health insurance or dental care if their child truly could not pay for these important expenses.

When the issue is whether to subsidize a young adult who is in limbo over a job or in a lower-paying job, parents had more questions than answers. For those at the younger end of the spectrum, the options are dazzling. Tad noted: 'They don't really know when they're making the right choices. I think possibilities are wonderful but if you have a whole range of them to select from, it just becomes even more difficult. To make a good choice requires a great deal of maturity. We're saying, "Don't just take a job because it will pay the bills and advance your career." But they're not sure what they're going to like. They're not even sure what clothes they want to put on the next day sometimes, and you're telling them, "Love your job. You know I love mine, I hope you love yours." I think it's a very big frightening world for them.'

Add the mixed messages we give to the fact that there are so many choices today, especially with jobs and fields that didn't exist for us. Dale remarks, 'I think I would encourage them to make changes and move around. The perfect time to do that is when they are young adults. Better to explore and experiment when you're young. I believe this in principle but I found it hard as a parent. I have mixed feelings. On the one hand we encouraged our children to find their bliss. But there comes a point when you say, "Enough already. Just take a job and pay your bills." Because there's also the issue of helping them become responsible for their own lives while supporting them or contributing in a major way. It is important that we don't give them sufficient money so they suck their thumbs emotionally. How do we help them become responsible adults even while we allow them to search, and how are we going to be a part of that? If we're contributing financially then it becomes a complicated emotional issue.'

Intellectually we tell our children to be true to themselves, to enjoy life before they have too many responsibilities. But emotionally, parents may resent their child for not working while they work hard to pay their bills. Renee admits, 'I found myself upset at times when the children would take great vacations, while I was working long hours to have extra money available for them. Money issues from both sides do cloud the relationship. The key is to continually talk together and clarify each person's needs and expectations. These are complicated issues and it's not easy.'

The value of subsidizing a young adult came up often as parents questioned whether it encourages them to remain stuck in a difficult financial situation. One parent called it 'our dirty little secret'. She felt embarrassed for anyone to know they were subsidizing their son to live away from home. She explained, 'Dick lives in New York City and makes about $20,000. Even in a very modest studio apartment he can't pay his bills on that salary so we've been giving him monthly supplements. But I wonder if that allows him to stay stuck in this low-paying job. Maybe if we withdrew our support, he would have to find a better job.' In the discussion, Terri elaborated that Dick really was trying to move up the ladder but it takes time and a lot of networking. With this clarification, Terri realized they weren't promoting lack of motivation. They were being supportive, financially and emotionally, to Dick at this time.

Deirdre's parents decided to subsidize her income due to very different circumstances but, as with Dick's situation, the intent is to strengthen and empower the young adult's life. Deirdre has learning disabilities and Attention Deficit Hyperactivity Disorder (ADHD). Prone to depression, poor judgment and impulsive behavior, Deirdre has had a troubled history. There have been confrontations and tension between Deirdre and her parents for many years. As a student, she was unmotivated. School was a struggle, from getting up in the morning, to attending each day and completing assignments.

When all her friends went off to college, her plan was to attend a local community college and work part-time. After one semester, she failed her courses. She was constantly arguing with her parents who felt she was staying out too late, skipping classes and not taking responsibility for her life. Years of confrontations and what they viewed as lack of maturity wore her parents down. Deirdre kept telling them she was 19 and wanted to be on her own. They decided to help her find a decent, affordable apartment and offered her a monthly allotment on which to live for six months. Together Deirdre and her parents estimated a budget for rent, food, car payments and personal expenses. They signed an agreement that Deirdre would have their support for six months, giving her time to find a full-time job. At the end of six months, she was expected to be on her own. Her parents agreed to help with any large emergency expenses providing Deirdre was helping herself.

This kind of financial support (with variations, depending on the individual situation) may be considered when the young adult is immature and/or hindered in some way from being fully responsible. Some young people are not prepared to support themselves as they lack any professional training or direction. Others are very immature and make poor choices, going from one bad relationship to another, losing jobs, having car accidents. These young adults are a particular challenge to parents who are trying to be encouraging and supportive. While you might have to be more active in suggesting options and providing some limits, it is especially important to avoid lectures and long, repetitive comments about all the things you feel your daughter or son is doing wrong.

For many families it is a dilemma to know when to give financial assistance. Joan related a time in her life when she and her husband were particularly stretched themselves. One daughter was just finishing her PhD and was in the process of finding a job. She came to them for help, saying she didn't have money to pay for rent and needed to borrow $250 a month. They helped her for several months but it meant they were unable to pay some of their own bills. Finally they told their daughter they could no longer afford to help her out. She began to budget and when she got a job, was able to start saving money. Joan felt it changed her daughter's life when she was forced to be more accountable.

Other parents talked about children who chose careers they loved but, in today's world, did not make a lot of money. One parent suggested there's no right or wrong, no good or bad. 'Whatever you're doing with your kids in your situation, it needs to work for you. I would suggest there's no reason for any of us to feel guilty because I also subsidize my kids willingly and lovingly. If I have the money, I can help them. If my son is making only $22,000 and can't go out with his buddies to have a beer and pizza, then I want to help him out. I don't think that's right or wrong.'

When we do help our young adults, they may have mixed feelings. On the one hand they appreciate the help, maybe even rely on it. But on the other hand it may create feelings of dependence – I'm still a kid needing money and daddy's help – or guilt. Peter acknowledges, 'I feel my parents are very supportive financially and they always say, "You don't have to worry about money until you get started" but I still feel guilty that I have to live off them, even though I have no other means. They're supporting me and they want me to experience this volunteer teaching program, but every day I still feel guilty about it and will do until I start making my own money.'

Walter appreciated that his parents kept advising him to find work that would make him happy. Even though he described them as wealthy, all the time they were helping him he kept wondering how he could ever repay them. He felt very indebted and uncomfortable. Finally he realized what he could do to compensate his parents for their support. He said, 'I learned to take what they're giving me and learn from them, so I can do it with my own children someday.' Obviously if we can afford to help our children and choose to do so, it is important to do it graciously to minimize the possibility of guilt or bad feelings. If we can't afford even a small gift or a loan, it is better to state that than to give and be sending direct or indirect messages of anger or martyrdom.

A very different message regarding finances that makes young adults very uncomfortable results from hostilities between divorced parents. Children of divorced parents often feel like a ball bounced back and forth when it comes to paying for certain items. Each parent tells their child to ask the other. The child has to approach each parent and is often refused by both, or one will resentfully provide the funds, making the child feel guilty for needing what might, to another family, be a very reasonable request. That parent's anger toward the former spouse gets misdirected to the child – an uncomfortable situation for all involved. As before, a kind, sensitive approach on the part of both parents would prove quite constructive.

For discussion:
- If you are currently giving your young adult money on a regular basis, is it done with the intent to control their choices or to be supportive?
- How could you talk together about these funds to ensure the expectations and terms are clear to everyone?

Equal treatment

Money by itself or as a metaphor can cause conflict between siblings when one feels another gets preferential treatment. Edward, the builder who was refused a loan by his father, has a long list of gifts and financial aid his parents have given his sister and her family, which they have not given to him or his children. When one sibling repeatedly gets large amounts of money and expensive gifts but the others do not, this inequality can be internalized as feeling unloved or unworthy. Inequality can also cause huge rifts between siblings and/or parents and young adult.

While we try to be sensitive to the needs of each of our children, short of keeping detailed ledgers, it is hard to keep it exactly the same. Brad felt resentful for years about the fact that his parents provided a car for his sisters, while he bought his own car. Finally he talked to his parents about these feelings. They reminded him that he chose to buy himself the car but that they had paid for its insurance and repairs for more than six years. Since he was working on Wall Street and needed suits for his job, his birthday gifts for two years were five times the amount his sisters received because he needed a business wardrobe and they did not.

Each family finds its own way of equalizing the help. The Waters resolved the fairness issue in this way: 'We give our kids a fair amount of money. They are basically affluent. They have a lot of dead relatives so they have some money of their own and it's in their name, and they know we really don't expect them to do anything with it but save it for a down payment on a house or something similar. All three of them get exactly the same amount of money, even though their needs are not the same. Melissa needs every cent of it to get through living in New York. Al is about two-thirds of the way saving for a Harley Davidson, and Andrew has saved every last penny. Because their work ethic is so strong, all three of them work all the time. It's not about being lazy. Melissa, who should watch her money carefully because she's living in such a high rent area, probably budgets the least. Andrew only goes to the movies once a week and hardly ever goes out for dinner – he's going to end up this wealthy miser. Melissa, at the end of the month or the end of the year, will say, "Oh my God, I hope I can make it" and she'll figure it out. But they all know from year to year how much income to expect. It never changes. This is what it is and has been since they got out of college.'

Parents' feelings, either for the child or the situation, can affect financial decisions and differential treatment. Peter's mother was upset when his sister got her law degree and chose to work for a non-profit agency rather than accept a high-paying position in a prestigious law firm. Although Peter is a teacher with a lower income, his mother tells him she doesn't worry about his future ability to support himself. He understands her concerns stem from her own experience when his parents divorced, and she did not have a way to meet her financial needs.

The Carrolls are a blended family. Allen married Leigh when she was divorced and had two daughters. He helped raise the girls and together they had two sons. The girls as teenagers went to live with their father. Although he loves them and they call him dad, Allen feels closer to his own natural sons. He also feels financially obligated to help them more as the girls have another family. Therefore when it came time to draw up wills, he decided to leave his share of their estate only to his sons, knowing his wife would divide her share equally into four parts.

His decision caused turmoil in the family. His wife was very hurt that he was excluding her daughters, and the daughters felt this position meant their stepfather never really loved them. Allen eventually modified his will to give the majority of his estate to his sons and divide the rest equally between the two girls. Short of leaving everything equally divided four ways, this situation is full of potential resentments and conflicts. There are no easy answers, as this excerpt from one parent discussion group indicates:

Terri: *I have a question that has to do with something you said. Do you feel that you have to treat all your children the same way?*
Betty: *No!*
Terri: *Because you said that you're giving each the same amount of money. I personally wouldn't. I would help the one who needed it and I wouldn't give anything to the others. I know that's very unfair. How do most people feel? Do you think you should treat all the children the same way?*
Tad: *Well, I don't think so. I do think you should help the one that needs to be helped, but I think you have to give the others something else.*

Dorothy: *I don't know. It's a hard issue.*

Tad: *Money is an almost separate issue.*

Terri: *It's very fraught.*

Tad: *I have two brothers and my mother just died and left all her money to the one she thought needed it. And he doesn't need it anymore. Now we're not speaking.*

Terri: *Money is a really heavy issue, I think.*

Tad: *I absolutely agree.*

Terri: *Money can create tremendous conflict.*

Dale: *Beware the curse of money!*

We all want to feel loved and important. Since money is one way people feel loved or appreciated, it becomes important for parents to be thoughtful in their giving; loving, honest and direct in discussing their decisions.

For discussion:

- How have you addressed the issue of fairness in your family?

Helping young adults to learn about money

We asked young adults in our discussion groups whether they felt well educated about financial issues like investments, mortgages and insurance. We wondered if their parents had prepared them for the real world in this way. We got a unanimous 'No'. Amy has an unusual situation but speaks for many: 'I think that's really, really important because you never know when you are going to need that information. When I was younger, my parents got divorced. They didn't want to talk about money because they didn't want me to know about their problems. Then, about a year ago, my mother passed away and I got a trust fund. I have an executor for my trust fund so I have all this money but I have no idea what to do with it. I have no idea where I'm going to put it when I'm 23. It would have been so helpful to have had some conversations about money. I still have no idea about leases or accounting. I don't know how to keep a checkbook. I don't even know where to keep savings. I know how to use the Mac card – I know it's green and you can buy stuff with it. Basically if I don't see it in front of my face, if it's done electronically, I just have no idea how to deal with it. That's a really bad thing because at college, you need to fill out applications for loans and money has to transfer. People don't write checks anymore. They have direct deposit, which is very confusing and you really need to understand it. Even during your senior year in high school, it's extremely important because you have to fill out loan applications.'

Walter is in his late 20s and had begun to accrue some savings. He asked his father, a very successful businessman, for suggestions. 'They never talk to me about finances. My dad avoided the topic. I wanted him to teach me about the stock market because I wanted to play around with some internet stocks. But I guess, as successful as he is, he doesn't want anybody else to ever take his advice and fail. I just couldn't get any answers at all, so I went out and made a lot of mistakes but I learned on my own.'

When our daughter and son-in-law started thinking about buying a house, we suggested they talk to our accountant to figure what they could afford and how much it would cost them. Instead they fell in love with a property and put a deposit down. As they got more into the process, we tried to advise them on financing and interest rates but they wanted to do it on their own. We realized that we had waited too long to teach them about IRAs (Individual Retirement Accounts), mortgages and insurance. As children get older, it seems to be a point of pride not to get advice from parents. We tried to explain that we wanted them to learn from some of our mistakes. The answer was they wanted to make their own mistakes. When our children are younger, they generally don't want to know about financial issues and how much they can spend. While it's not easy to find conducive opportunities, all the issues covered in this chapter warrant many direct, honest and informative discussions.

❤ There are many ways in which parents can be helpful to their young adults where financial issues are concerned. When we can't afford to give direct financial support, we can offer emotional support and advice. When we support or subsidize them for periods of time, it is important to spell out a clear agreement about how the money is to be spent and other terms. Young adults need our guidance and advice in areas of planning, investing, insurance, mortgages and loans. Since these topics can be rife with issues of dependence and independence, fairness and love, our communication skills need to be polished and refined to encourage frank, open discussions that avoid blame, hostility or mixed messages.

Chapter 6
Special needs

So far we have been suggesting a general shift in our parenting style to a more laid-back, hands-off approach in our young adult's decisions and choices. There are, however, special circumstances where we may need to be more actively involved in their lives. This chapter will explore how and when to be more directive if our grown children are having problems with substance abuse or emotional/psychological disturbances. You may have had to deal with one or more of these issues to some extent. Sometimes the problems are minor but our concerns are very real. We will read about a number of families who have faced these issues.

Substance abuse

Sometimes our young adult drinks too much. We may hear about the morning hangover, a wild night they had, or see them coming home drunk. Excessive drinking is always a parental concern. We know the grip alcoholism can have on a life. We may have experienced it directly in our family history or known someone whose life was touched unhappily by alcohol. Many young people view drinking as a part of socializing, a fun part. They rationalize that getting drunk is part of their youth culture, which they will one day outgrow. It is difficult for parents to hear about behavior so different from our own – behavior we don't understand and really dislike – and not want to change it. But our children know how we feel about excessive drinking so we don't have to keep repeating ourselves. Although we want to avoid lectures and repetitive negative comments, it is important to express our concerns and interest in casual conversation periodically. Our son or daughter may interpret lack of comments as synonymous with not caring or as tacit approval.

When your child lives at home and you see signs of excessive drinking, what is your responsibility? What are your rights? How can you address your concerns in a supportive way? If you sense their drinking is largely a social habit confined to weekends, you can express your concerns about their safety, getting home and being in control of how others behave toward them. If it impacts on the family because of noisy, middle-of-the-night arrivals, sleeping all day when the family has plans, or being a poor role model for younger siblings, these issues need to be aired in a sincere, concerned and non-blaming way.

When our child has a serious drinking problem, we may not be aware of it. Alcoholics (people who feel they need to drink to get through life although they may not need to drink every day) get very clever about hiding their addiction. Ken started to drink heavily while in high school. His friends were very concerned about his alcoholism but his parents seemed either unaware or unwilling to address the issue. When his parents did realize that he had a serious drinking problem at age 19, they often threatened that he would have to get help or move out, but they didn't follow it through. Ken said they would have the 'sit-down talks' but his parents' words would go in one ear and out the other. He stopped caring about what they thought; he only cared about getting drunk.

Although very bright and a talented writer, Ken worked during the day and drank at night. His friends watched him become an angry, morose young man, wasting his talents and isolating himself socially. This continued for a number of years. Finally, on a particularly destructive drinking binge, he passed out, only to awaken the next morning with his best friends and his parents seated around him. His friend had been pushing him for years to go for help. This particular

Sunday morning, his parents told him that they had had enough; that he either had to get help or he had to move out that day. Ken had been realizing for several months that he needed to stop drinking but when he saw his friends' and parents' faces, he realized he could no longer put them off with excuses and false promises. He told them he would go for help but that he would have to be locked up or it would never work. A week later, he entered an in-patient rehabilitation program, where he stayed for five months. Fortunately he had good insurance coverage from his job and was able to stay for an extended period of time until he trusted that he was ready to be on his own.

Ken noted that he had several friends with a drinking problem similar to his, whose parents forced them to go to rehab either in high school or shortly after. They only maintained their sobriety for several months and had since relapsed. His advice to parents was first to make sure that you don't let your son or daughter isolate themselves. He noted how he would go down into the basement to secretly drink alone and no one came down to check on him. He also isolated himself more and more from friends or any kind of social activities as he became more entrenched in his alcoholism. He didn't necessarily feel that his parents should have pushed him into a rehab treatment program earlier because he was not ready to admit and face his alcoholism. He predicted that it would have failed. Now, at 25, he's been attending AA meetings and has maintained his sobriety for over a year. He decided to take college courses and, with the encouragement of several professors in the English department, has started to submit his poems and short stories for publication. His friends note that he looks like a totally different person: eyes clear, gaze direct; he has a focus; he's interested in what others have to say; he is funny and full of plans for the future.

Sometimes we wait it out; in other circumstances we need to take action, as Ken's parents did. We cannot control our young adult's choices but we need to have some control over our own life. Paul started smoking pot sometime in high school. In his senior year he got caught selling drugs and was arrested. He received a fine, hours of community service and was sentenced to an in-patient rehab program. His parents attended the family meetings to learn how to deal with Paul's problems. For a while he stayed clear of drugs. Then, after he turned 18, he started getting involved again. By then he had finished high school but had no trade or direction. As an adopted child, he always had a lot of doubts about fitting in and being accepted. He is not very tall and not academically oriented – two factors that further hindered his self-esteem.

Paul's parents were very supportive. They continually told Paul how much they loved him and would help in any way they could. They took him for vocational counseling. The tests suggested a strong interest in cooking and restaurant management. This led to an apprenticeship in a local restaurant, where the staff found him very amiable and eager to learn. He started to feel like an important part of the team and took on more and more responsibility. His parents learned that Paul would continue to be tempted by his old friends and by drugs unless he had skills and direction, which in turn would bolster his self-esteem. They also learned to ask him directly how he was feeling, how he was doing without using drugs. In the past they avoided the topic because he got so angry and defensive. As quiet, private people, they didn't talk much about feelings but they learned to reach out to Paul and most of the time he was responsive and appreciative.

When our child is still living at home, it is easier to set limits and have some input. We met Mary in earlier chapters. Since many of her friends were under age, her parents felt comfortable visiting the family room periodically unannounced to discourage drinking in their home. They set earlier hours for friends to be out of the house and curfews for Mary to be home at weekends. You can use the privilege of living at home as leverage when you want your young adult to seek help. However, once you take a stand you have to be able to follow this through.

Beth and Ed, both previously married and divorced, moved in together when her son Eric was 21 and living with some friends in an apartment. One year later, shortly after they married, Eric asked to move in with them, ostensibly to save money. Ed got along well with him so they didn't foresee any problems. It quickly became apparent that there was a huge problem as Eric was addicted to cocaine. They insisted he go to a rehab program, which he did for four weeks. Like Paul's parents, Beth and Ed participated in the family group meetings. When Eric returned home, he stayed clear of drugs. He also expressed interest in getting computer skills, so Beth took a home equity loan from the bank and paid his tuition for a three-month program in computer technology, all the while keeping her fingers crossed that he would continue to be drug-free. Eric graduated with high honors and had no trouble finding a job with an excellent salary.

After a few weeks, Ed commented to Beth that he thought Eric was using again. He pointed out the bloodshot eyes and erratic hours. Beth accused Ed of being too hard on Eric, not giving him a chance, not believing in him. He countered that she was too naive and easy on Eric. As the weeks continued, the arguments between Beth and Ed accelerated to the point where they started talking about a divorce. Ed reminded Beth that they had to keep their agreement with Eric to maintain credibility and help him take responsibility. If he did drugs again, he would have to move out. She began to waver, feeling she just couldn't throw her own son out if he were having problems. Finally, after Eric disappeared on a three-day binge, during which time his boss called looking for him, Beth had to face the fact that Eric was using drugs again and his job was in jeopardy, as was her marriage.

Once he came home, she and Ed waited until he sobered up, then told him he was not sticking to his agreement and would have to leave.

He tried to deny it at first but they held firm. They helped him pack up his clothes and personal items, then waited for his friend to come and pick him up. After he left, they had the locks changed. Eric eventually moved in with his father, who was always more permissive when it came to family rules. Beth doesn't know if her son will be able to get back in control but she realized there was nothing more she could do. She had accompanied him to counseling, paid a lot of money for his tuition, talked with him and supported him for over a year. She could not rescue Eric. Now she had to put energy into saving her marriage and her own emotional well-being.

Along with the worry for Eric's safety and future, Beth wrestled with the demons of guilt and 'what ifs'. She blamed herself for Eric's addiction, trying to second-guess in hindsight if she had stayed in her first marriage for too long and should have got a divorce sooner. When our grown children make poor choices, we cannot take on responsibility for their behavior. Nor can we take all the credit when they are successful! By letting go, we actually empower our children to become adults. Beth and Ed kept in touch with Eric, seeing him periodically and talking to him regularly. They conveyed their love and interest so he didn't feel abandoned or rejected. He had to leave because he didn't keep his agreement to stay off drugs. The last we heard, Beth and Ed were taking ballroom dance lessons, planning a trip to California and building a new home. Eric was continuing to struggle with his addiction.

For discussion:

- Does your young adult have an alcohol or drug problem?
- If there are any concerns over drinking or drug abuse, what options do you have?
- For young adults, how would you want your parents to handle this with you?

Emotional/psychological disturbances

Everyone goes through some rough times emotionally. It is painful as a parent to watch our child, at any age, be depressed and unhappy. When our son or daughter is technically an adult, it is so confusing to know what our role is. If the unhappiness is a reaction to a specific event, such as the break-up of a relationship or problem at work, the best thing we can do is to listen empathetically and then offer assurance that they can work through this unhappy time. By really listening, we are not trying to tell them what to do, take over the situation, or belittle the way they already handled the situation. Most likely, they need to vent their feelings, hear themselves outloud and pull from within their own resources to begin to heal or resolve the problem. That is empowering to our child, and far more helpful than trying to fix it ourselves, although it may not feel that way. By assuring them that they will work it through, we offer hope and faith in their abilities.

We can be more emotionally detached when the problem is situational and we know it can be handled with time. Some young adults have such severe problems that direct intervention is necessary. Our role may range from urging our child to get professional help to being involved in the treatment, and in some cases actively supervising their care, as we will illustrate with a number of family stories. Although we may be very involved, it is especially important to be sensitive to our child's feelings that they are an adult. Even when they acknowledge needing our help, they are conscious of their age, so it is a particularly difficult balancing act to be helpful yet respectful of their need for some control.

When therapy is useful

For most of us, an experience with counseling may be very helpful at some point in our lives. While nowadays there is far less stigma attached to seeking professional help, many misconceptions remain. Some still believe that people only seek help if they are hearing voices or so massively depressed that they cannot get out of bed. Others fear they will automatically be placed on medication. And to most, the process of finding the right therapist seems daunting.

Obviously, as professionals who have earned their living as psychotherapists for 30 years, we strongly believe in the process. We have seen thousands of people benefit from some kind of therapeutic encounter, sometimes in only one or two sessions, although the process of change usually takes longer. We often explain to people that therapy is very much like taking a self-improvement course. It is a way of learning more about yourself, and finding ways to change ineffective behaviors into strong coping skills. It is life-enhancing, not demeaning.

We have sought counseling for ourselves at times when we felt stymied or upset and couldn't be objective enough to find our way out of a situation. For each of our children, there have been times in their young adulthood where they have gone for sessions. When one of them gets very bogged down, one or more of us will find a supportive way to suggest that they go and see Jane, a warm and truly gifted therapist in New York City. We also went for some family sessions, which were extremely helpful. Jane has fondly become incorporated into our family, almost like a special aunt who we can visit and talk with as needed.

As parents, we can be less emotionally involved and more objective if we get our young adult to see a therapist. But it is important to make the suggestion in a supportive way, waiting for an opening or a better time when our child might be receptive. Don't be surprised if the first response is one of anger or denial. You can plant the suggestion, then it is up to them to think about it. If they are not ready, no amount of prodding will make them go or adopt a receptive attitude. Sometimes it is a relief to the young adult to have therapy as a support. Reactions may vary widely. If you are going to make the suggestion, it is also important that you decide in advance if you are willing to help pay for any sessions if your child's insurance will not cover treatment. It can be expensive for a young person to see a private therapist and pay the full fee. For a college student, the health services on campus offer counselors and that is a good place to start. You can find your local area's community services in the phone book, through a hospital, a religious organization, a university, or Family Services. Ask your doctor or friends that you know have been in therapy – they are also good referral sources.

We may also wish to seek professional help for ourselves. One couple came for just one session to voice concerns over a grandchild. After giving the family background and descriptions of the troublesome behaviors, we explored their options. They began the session by acknowledging there might not be anything they could do as grandparents. By the end of the session, they formulated a strategy where the parent with the most comfortable relationship with their daughter would wait for an appropriate moment to share their concerns and suggest that the parents go with the child for some therapy before the problems get worse. These bright people realized the risk that their daughter and son-in-law might be offended but felt it was worth that possibility. Together we role-played some ways the parents might broach the subject. Other parents have sought counseling for themselves as they evolve in this vibrant stage of life. With the right therapist, sensitive and responsive to your needs, counseling can be enlightening and even fun at times.

For discussion:

- Do you see signs that you or your young adult might benefit from professional help?
- List ways you would go about finding a therapist.

Eating disorders

Emily seemed like the all-American girl. She got excellent grades, always had many friends, was attractive, and never gave her parents any trouble. When she came home for summer break after her freshman [first] year at college, her parents noticed a change in her attitude. She seemed silent and withdrawn, irritable when they made just light conversation with her. Then her mother began noticing some strange marks around Emily's bathroom sink and toilet. Her suspicions aroused, she asked to talk with Emily and questioned her directly about her concerns. Reluctantly, Emily admitted she had become obsessed with her appearance while at school and was vomiting five to six times a day to control her weight. Her mother immediately wanted to make an appointment for counseling but Emily balked, saying she could work it out herself. Mrs T knew nothing about eating disorders. She agreed to give Emily four weeks to stop vomiting and return to her easygoing personality, or she would take her for therapy.

During the four weeks, Mrs T did a lot of reading about eating disorders, learning that they are one of the most intractable problems to treat as the person becomes obsessed with looking good and being thin out of all proportion to their actual appearance. Mrs T watched for signs that Emily was able to control her vomiting but found the opposite to be true. By the time four weeks had passed, Mrs T had set up an appointment with a therapist specializing in eating disorders. After talking with Emily alone, the therapist invited the parents to join them. He proposed a plan of treatment and suggested how they could be helpful. He encouraged Emily to tell her parents what she needed from them. She acknowledged that she wanted them to ask about her urge to vomit, to talk about her feelings and how she thought the treatment was going. Emily had perceived their lack of questioning as a lack of interest in her. But she was equally clear that she did not want them watching her as she ate or commenting on how much she was eating. Mrs T wanted to point out when Emily reached for a second or third helping, believing that would help Emily eat less and therefore have less need to purge. Emily heard that comment as validation that she was indeed fat, so she asked her parents not to question her eating habits. It was helpful, as the therapy continued, to clarify what were Emily's individual issues to work on, and how her parents could be helpful. Fortunately, since Emily was still a student, she was covered under her family's insurance plan. Emily was able to continue with counseling once she was back at school. Her parents were reluctant to let her return, fearing she would relapse into the purging behavior once back in the environment where it began. They worked out an agreement with Emily to include several checks and balances to monitor her progress. She would have to drop out of school and return home for intensive treatment if they found she was still purging.

Taylor struggled with bulimia but she didn't acknowledge it to anyone until she graduated from college and was living on her own for one year. Although she was living in another city, it became apparent to her mom that Taylor was not doing well. Sometimes she didn't answer her phone or return calls for days at a time and she sounded very depressed. Taylor had found work as a substitute teacher but that was not steady employment and she had no benefits. Her mom drove to see her when a particularly long time went by with no contact. She found Taylor disheveled, weak, with no food in her apartment and no money. Eileen called her husband to arrange for a consultation with a psychiatrist and drove Taylor back home. The psychiatrist told the parents that Taylor was not only severely depressed but had been bulimic for many years and probably was in some physical distress as a result. He recommended immediate hospitalization. Eileen and Tom were dumbfounded. They wanted to help their daughter but without any insurance they were told hospitalization alone would cost about $30,000. Their incomes were modest and they had other children preparing to go to college. The only way they could help was to borrow from their retirement fund.

Eileen and Tom were able to pay for psychiatric hospitalization at a major medical center in another state for six weeks. Taylor made progress but her therapists wanted her to get an apartment and stay near the hospital to continue her treatment as an outpatient. Her parents spent another $20,000 for her outpatient care and living expenses. When she and her therapists agreed she was ready, she moved back home with a plan to set up continued treatment with a local therapist and to look for a job so she could eventually move out and be self-supporting. After several months at home, her parents were dismayed to learn she was bingeing and purging again. At that point they expressed their love and concern but also told Taylor they could no longer afford to pay for therapy. They had exhausted their funds and she would have to find some way to work on these issues herself. It was heartbreaking to Eileen and Tom to watch their daughter have these problems. But the reality was they had severely depleted their own savings and could not continue to do so. And they felt in some way they were enabling Taylor to be dependent and not take more responsibility to resolve her issues.

Whether our young adult is fighting an addiction with drugs or alcohol, or having psychological problems like an eating disorder, most parents will find it hard to understand these behaviors. They may view them simplistically, expecting their child to just be able to stop in a short period of time, or change without significant professional intervention. It helps to do some reading, attend group meetings, or talk with other parents to gain insight into the tenacious grip these behaviors have. Parents also tend to persist in blaming themselves and often become seriously depressed themselves, to some extent taking on the burden of their son's or daughter's problem. That is why a support group or professional counseling can be very important to the parents as well as the individual.

A note of caution: the internet can be a valuable resource for information regarding treatment options, understanding the problems, and finding a support network. Be discriminating as not all information is accurate and/or applicable to your situation.

The onset of acute illness

Like Emily, both Rob and Wendy seemed like typical kids. At some point in college both had breakdowns and required hospitalization. Diagnosed with the onset of adult schizophrenia, their symptoms are similar but their paths suggest the different ways parents might be involved in their young adult's care.

After her breakdown and hospitalization, Wendy tried to return to college but was unable to function there. She returned home and continued with treatment so that her medication could be monitored to decrease her paranoia, confusion and depression. Once she was stabilized, she enrolled at a local college and took a reduced load. Her mother found that Wendy had trouble organizing her time and thoughts so she began to help Wendy with her studies. Although it required a chunk of her time each day, Mrs D decided it was worth it because it gave Wendy a goal and a semblance of normalcy to be in college. Mrs D had shifted when Wendy left for college, beginning to find interests and activities for her own personal development. When Wendy became ill, she chose to shift again to being actively involved in Wendy's daily life. The system is working for both of them now. No one can anticipate what further shifts will take place in the future.

Rob and his family went a different route. When he fell apart and returned home, he was very angry and difficult to live with. His parents would try to give suggestions. They found jobs for him to do, as he was very skillful. Rob would always end up in an argument with them because he wanted to do things one way and they had something different in mind. Because of his paranoia, he felt they were constantly criticizing him and treating him like a young child. Due to the continual tension, Rob felt he wanted to be on his own. His parents agreed but realized he couldn't function independently at that time. They did some research and connected with a psychiatric clinic. Rob's therapist there put the wheels in motion. Rob was categorized as disabled so he qualified for Medicaid, which enabled him to get coverage for treatment and medication. He was placed in a group home, where he has lived for several years.

When Rob began the program, he was under constant supervision and had a lot of individual and group therapy. His parents attended weekly group family sessions and were in touch with his caseworker, occasionally having sessions with her and Rob. As Rob has progressed, he has moved from a dorm room to an apartment with one room-mate – to his own 'bachelor pad'. The amount of time spent in therapy has been reduced so Rob can have a full-time job. He enjoys the companionship of the other young people in the program and is proud of his responsibilities at work. He still needs the safety net of his therapy sessions and caseworker, which helps him navigate the waters that come with chronic depression and paranoid ideation.

A year ago Rob's father was transferred to another state. His parents were extremely worried that selling the family home and moving out of the area might undermine Rob's progress to date. He was used to going home for visits and seeing his parents regularly. His parents considered taking Rob with them but were worried about disrupting his program, where he was doing so well and was receiving a lot of support. To their surprise and relief, and Rob's pride, he seems to have become more independent, as if he were able to push into a higher level of functioning once he was truly on his own. At some point he may move, either to live with his parents or nearby, depending on his needs at the time. For now, Rob's parents have found a way to lead their lives but keep a watchful eye on their son. They try to come back every one to two months to meet with Rob and his counselor, and attend the family sessions. And they have tremendous respect for the efforts he has made to pull his life together, a respect that is reflected in the way they talk with Rob, ask him about his feelings, and remember to consult him if any decisions have to be made. Rob feels he is been being treated in his program and by his parents as a young adult and this gives him great comfort as well as incentive to continue.

Care for those with chronic illness

When he was a toddler, Michael seemed different to his parents. Douglas and Lynn had him evaluated and learned he had Attention Deficit Hyperactivity Disorder (ADHD) to a severe degree and significant learning disabilities. With medication, his impulsivity was somewhat controlled but he had difficulty focusing if there were too many distractions and often misread social cues, thinking someone was angry with him or staring at him. Michael had a very friendly social personality and was very loving at home. Once he finished high school, his parents wondered what to do with him. They heard of a supervised social group for young adults with learning or emotional difficulties. The purpose was to provide structured social activities for adults who might not fit in with the mainstream. As an outgrowth of this program, Douglas and Lynn learned about the possibility of independent living but with some overseeing of job connections and a psychiatrist to monitor his medication. They helped Michael move into an apartment and find a job in the shipping department of a nearby company. Michael made many friends through his group and developed a satisfying social life. His parents got to know his boss and his psychiatrist, who calls them if Michael stops taking his medication or is having a problem. They visit him monthly, taking him meals he can easily heat up. They also go over his expenses, helping him to balance his checkbook if needed.

This arrangement has worked well for more than 10 years. There were two occasions when Michael did something impulsive, once stopping his medication and another time quitting his job where they loved and accepted him. Both times he stopped eating and would not answer his phone or let his parents or friends in to check up on him. Lynn and Douglas had to go down to his apartment with a policeman and demand to be let in. Then they were able to get help for Michael and he got back on track. As Lynn and Douglas are ageing, they have put in place two alternative plans for someone to watch over Michael in the event of their deaths. With a lot of care and thought, Michael has been able to become semi-independent as an adult and his parents have found ways to be involved yet maintain some distance.

David, a widower for 10 years, has been raising his three children alone. Two children seem to have followed normal developmental patterns and not given him any major challenge. But his son Andrew was a concern even when he was little and his mother was still alive. By nature he was quiet – teachers described him as shy. His parents thought he would gradually become more comfortable around people as he got older. Now in his 20s, he spends most of his time at home, isolating himself even from his family. He is extremely uncomfortable around most people, answering in monosyllables if he answers at all. Different medications have been tried as well as therapy, which, although helpful in giving David some guidance, was uncomfortable and ultimately unproductive for Andrew.

In one discussion group, the other parents were talking about different problems they were having with their adult offspring. They generally concluded that their children would find their way in the world. David expressed his reservations for Andrew: 'In terms of trusting the future, I would think it doesn't always turn out okay. It's a very difficult world and I have one child with problems – learning disabilities and emotional problems – and I have a real concern that his life may not turn out okay. It's very, very difficult when you have a child who is an adult who really needs your help. There is a very fine line of how much help to give and how much to pull back. I think I really sort of took over at one point and gave him all the help I possibly could. In the last year, when he's been looking for a job, I stood back. Now I'm at a point where I don't think that is working and I may need to push him or actively go with him to apply for jobs, but it's very touchy when they are older. What's right? I think you have to watch very carefully but there are times when an adult child really does need help. He may be uncomfortable asking, and I just think you need to watch to decide when it is time to intervene.'

For discussion:

- What support system do you have to deal with your young adult's psychological problems?

What all these parents of young adults with addictions and psychological problems had to decide was some delicate balance point, unique to each situation, of when to intervene and when to pull back; how to provide support without infantilizing or demeaning their child; and how to find and use professional help and community resources as much as possible. In these situations, we need to talk to people who are supportive and objective because sometimes we can get too caught up in our need to rescue so that our judgment gets cloudy. Whether it is through a community-supported treatment program, private counseling, Alanon (for families of alcoholics in the U.S. – call 1-800-356-9996), or Families Anonymous (a U.S. support group for families with an emotionally troubled member – call 1-800-736-9805), it is important to get the support and advice of other parents and/or professionals who have experience with similar difficulties.

Chapter 7
Legal issues

When our young adult has legal issues, as with so many other areas of their life, we have choices in the degree to which we help. The help may range from listening, offering support, giving advice, or contacting a family friend who is a lawyer, to financial assistance and, in some cases, getting them to move back home. We can listen and offer our love and support, even when we feel our son or daughter demonstrates poor judgement. The 'zip your lips' philosophy goes a long way, especially after the truth has been revealed. Once someone has got in trouble, we especially need to remember to stick to the issue at hand. To say, 'I told you so' or to make derogatory comments such as 'You're a loser', 'You are so irresponsible', 'You will never grow up', and so on, are destructive behaviors, both to the relationship and to our young adult's self-conception, which is already shaken.

It is easier to be a good parent when we are enjoying our daughter or son because they are doing what we expect. When they get into legal difficulty, it takes a lot of effort to zip our lips and just address the issue at hand. We constantly need to remind ourselves that it is their problem, not ours. It is their responsibility to deal with, not ours. As we have stressed throughout this book, we are the consultant, not the boss.

When our young adult needs financial help, we may find we are not in a position to be supportive financially. Still, we've known parents who gave up their dream plans to remodel or take a trip, parents who came out of retirement and returned to work because they wanted to help and/or couldn't say no. In this section we will learn about four young adults who were arrested and how they and their parents dealt with it.

We will touch on the issues raised when a young adult gets divorced and needs help, ranging from financial support to housing and childcare. Then we will briefly raise possibilities resulting from our own legal issues – when parents divorce, setting up wills and choosing executors.

Involvement with the police

In previous chapters we learned that Mary, 19, got arrested when her 17-year-old car passenger was found to have marijuana and an open beer can in his possession. Since he was considered under age, he got a lecture and was sent home. Mary was charged with possession of an illegal substance and being under age for drinking. She received a $750 fine, 60 hours of community service and one year on probation. At first Mary didn't even tell her parents about the arrest. She planned to pay off the fine herself, making monthly payments out of her paycheck. When she got fired and couldn't get another job right away, she had to ask her parents for the month's charges. Had her parents been told and/or if the sentence were more severe, her parents might have chosen to get a lawyer and try to reduce the charges. Since she opted to keep the arrest a secret initially, there was nothing they could do except make a plan for Mary to reimburse them.

Ben, Craig and Mike (all in their mid-20s) were on their way to pick up a fourth friend, Joe, to go mountain biking for the weekend. They weren't quite sure where Joe lived as Mike had only recently met him through work. Following Joe's somewhat vague directions on a dark Friday evening, Craig was having trouble finding his friend's house. He was driving slowly, especially at each intersection as the boys tried to read the signs. A policeman thought Craig was driving erratically and followed the car into Joe's driveway. At Joe's house, the officer ordered the three young men to get out of the car, then proceeded to search them and the car on suspicion of drugs. He found a bag of pot and some pipes in Craig's bag. All three were taken to the precinct and charged with possession.

Each young man decided to handle the situation differently. Ben and Craig immediately consulted their parents. Mike, on the other hand, was afraid to tell his parents. The charges carried a fine of $1,000, notice of arrest on his record, and one-year probation. Mike decided to accept what is called the first offender plea bargain. This means that he would pay the fine and accept the charges without contest. After six months of good behavior, the charges would be dropped and there would be no record. Craig and Ben felt they had been illegally searched and wanted to fight the charges. Craig's parents paid for a lawyer to represent their son. In his case, he also was in danger of losing his driver's license for six months and his job was dependent on his ability to drive to his customer's businesses. His case was heard individually and he was able to get the charges dropped. Ben felt it was his responsibility to deal with the situation financially, although he had his parents' emotional support. He met with a lawyer who charged him $3,000. He did not do as well as Craig did in the disposition. Ben got a reduced fine and lesser charges due to a plea bargain in which he agreed to plead guilty to a municipal disorder. Although his primary concern was to avoid a record of arrest, he was upset that the judge did not accept his premise that it was an illegal search and he should not be held responsible for another's behavior. In essence, he was punished for being in the company of others who possessed drugs. It was a bitter and costly lesson for him to learn. But it has made him more cautious about his own behavior and choice of friends.

Craig was open with his parents, who were willing to pay his legal fees. They could afford to help financially and wanted to be supportive. While Ben's parents were emotionally supportive, they would not have given Ben money for legal expenses had he asked. They strongly believed that Ben, as an adult, needed to accept the consequences of his choices. If you choose to socialize with friends who take drugs, you may find yourself in trouble. While it was hard as parents to see Ben struggle with this issue, they believed it had the potential to be a learning experience for Ben. The parents of Craig and Ben based their decisions on what they believed to be best for their son and their family. Both approaches are valid.

For discussion:
- Do you have a policy, should your young adult get into trouble with the law?
- Would your young adult know what approach to expect in your family?

When the young adult divorces

When our young adult's marriage ends in divorce, we may be sad, relieved, or happy. Certainly it is a difficult time in our daughter's or son's life as their plans and dreams for the future are disrupted. Even when the relationship was stressful and antagonistic or, for some, abusive, there is a lot of sadness for the death of the future as they had imagined it. There are practical issues of dividing up furniture and other assets, custody decisions if children are involved. Another decision becomes where to live if your young adult is the one to leave or can't afford to stay in the couple's home alone. Moving back in with you temporarily might be the best option. And, of course, money or financial support becomes an issue: a lawyer needs a retainer fee that can be several thousand dollars or more; moving costs money; paying bills becomes a problem without a second income; and unforeseen expenses. What's a parent to do?

When Susan decided to leave her marriage, it was a very emotional time for her. She knew she had been unhappy for a long time. She knew

Jim was abusive and had a drinking problem. They went for counseling together once Jim realized she was serious about leaving. Although he made many promises to change, Susan wasn't sure she could believe it and doubted she loved him. Still, she was getting contradictory advice from friends and family: some blaming her, some telling her he deserved one more chance, others telling her she was young with no children and should definitely get divorced. In this state of emotional turmoil, Susan arrived at her mom's two-bedroomed condo where she lived with her two younger sisters. She cried for several hours, then fell asleep on the living room couch. Two months later, she was still there. She decided to seek a divorce but had no money saved for a deposit on an apartment. She and Jim had purchased a townhouse but it would be sometime before she could get back her share of the money they had put down. Together they had run up a sizable credit card debt, which they agreed to split.

Her family was not happy to have her living in the only public gathering place in the tiny condo. Nor did they appreciate having her cat as well as her clothes in piles on the living room floor. But her mom didn't feel comfortable telling her she had to leave when there was nowhere else to go, nor did she have any extra money put aside that she could give Susan for an apartment. Susan ended up staying there for five months until she saved some money and was able to find an apartment she could afford.

Other parents might have handled the situation differently, either lending Susan the money for a deposit on an apartment or telling her she had to find a place to stay, even if it meant staying in her townhouse with Jim until it was sold. There is no right way, nor can we usually plan for these occurrences. We deal with them when they come up in what seems like the best way at the time. In making that decision, we need to consider not only what is helpful to our young adult but also what is important to ourselves, any other children or family living in our home, and our current obligations. Without being hard-hearted, merely acknowledging realities, there may come a time for many families when the circumstances of one child does not have to take precedence over our own and/or other family members' needs.

Joe didn't have time to explore his options. One evening he got into an argument with his wife. As it escalated, she pushed him and he pushed her back. She called 911 and told the police her husband had hit her. They suggested he spend the night in a motel so they could both cool down. He left and found out the next day she had filed a restraining order against him on false charges she made up. He could not go home. After a few days in a motel room, his wife made it clear she wanted a divorce and she would not allow him to visit the children. It was going to be a long, nasty battle. Joe knew he would need to find a good lawyer and a place to live. He had money for neither. Calling his parents, who lived in another state, he learned that they had never liked his wife or the way she treated him but hadn't wanted to cause problems between them so they kept quiet. Now they were all too happy to help him.

The next weekend, they drove up with extra linens, pots, utensils and lamps, plus their checkbook. They had transferred funds from the savings account, which they had been planning to use for a cruise trip on their 30th wedding anniversary. Instead they helped Joe find an apartment, paid the first and last month's rent and security deposit, plus $2,000 more to use as a retainer fee for his lawyer. Joe felt guilty taking the money for his parents' dream vacation but accepted the fact that they truly wanted to help. He promised to pay them back as soon as possible. Had his parents been unable to help or chosen not to, Joe might have stayed in an inexpensive motel, or found a room in a private home that took in boarders. Young adults are resilient and he would have survived somehow, but his parents' assistance provided more comfort and flexibility during this difficult time.

For discussion:

- What would you be prepared to do, should your married young adult want to leave their marriage?

When parents divorce

A startling percentage of marriages end after 20 years or more together. It has become an all-too-familiar scenario. As the children leave home, the parents' marital difficulties become exacerbated, as if the children were the glue without which the relationship cannot survive. The problems may have been chronic and obvious to the children while growing up or they may come as a shock. One parent seems to change, pursuing other interests, staying away more and eventually telling their partner, 'I don't love you anymore.' We will explore this scenario from the parents' perspective in chapter 9. Here we want to look at ways to make this easier on the young adult children. Because no matter how old the 'children' may be, even if married and long on their own, they usually find the divorce of their parents to be a painful experience that continues for a long time.

Sheila was married and the eldest of four children. When she learned that her parents were separating, she was totally devastated. Her siblings were equally distraught. While she didn't always like the way her father treated her mother and she heard them arguing that he was never home enough, she never expected them to actually separate. Her family had always been very close. Even now that they each lived in a different city, she talked on the phone to at least one of her siblings as well as her mother and grandparents on a daily basis. Both sides had a large extended family and they shared holidays together. Sheila's family was her security base, her foundation. Newly married herself, it frightened her that what seemed like a pretty good relationship could fall apart. She started obsessing over her own relationship, over-reacting with fear whenever she and her husband had a disappointment or he seemed distracted and inattentive. It put a strain on their relationship as she examined every interaction for signs that their marriage was in trouble.

Traditional holiday gatherings became a nightmare. There were tugs of war over where the children would go for Christmas and Easter dinner. When her mother hosted the family (now it was only her side) the meal resembled a smaller version of previous family rituals. But when it was her father's turn, Sheila was called upon in her small apartment to be the organizer, hostess and cook. Her father would show up as a guest.

When, two years after the divorce, her father announced that he was engaged and planned to marry, it caused another seismic shake-up in the family structure. He married a woman 20 years younger than him – only five years older than Sheila. Her stepmother became pregnant and gave birth around the same time that Sheila and her husband had their first child. So Sheila had a newborn daughter and a baby sister, and her dad had a granddaughter the same age as his child. Sheila still shakes her head and comments, 'It's just not what it's supposed to be.' Life is what's happening while you are busy making plans.

When parents divorce in midlife, their adult children will experience some fallout. While each young adult will react differently depending on personality, circumstances and family dynamics, parents need to be sensitive to the issues it creates. Research has proven that children of all ages deal with divorce best when the parents can maintain a co-operative front. That means refraining from negative remarks and facial expressions that are critical, hostile or belittling of the other parent. Children need to love and have a relationship with both parents to the extent possible. A child is composed of parts from each parent so to denigrate a parent is to denigrate part of your child. If there is a problem with their parent's behavior – for example, dad doesn't seem to make an effort to keep in touch or mom keeps taking dad to court for more money – young adults usually sense what is happening and decide how they feel about the situation. They don't want to hear mom saying, 'Your dad doesn't really care about you anymore, he's too busy making money' or hear dad complain that mom is such a selfish person.

Also children don't want to be put in the middle as the message-bearer: 'Next time you see your mother, tell her I need last year's tax returns.' If you have business to take care of, do it directly by phone, mail, in person or through your lawyer if necessary, but not through the children. It catches them in the web of hostilities and divided loyalties. One family has found the ideal compromise. Initially when her husband left, Peggy was very angry and bitter. The parents fought over each holiday, birthday and special event. The children were asked to pick which parent they wanted to be with, or were ordered to go to one or the other, always feeling torn that the other parent was left out. Eventually Peggy's ex-husband remarried and as the years went by, Peggy decided it was really in the best interest of her children to become friendly with her ex and his new wife, who by all accounts appeared genuinely interested in her children. All parties were agreeable to spending holidays together rather than having to alternate the special times. Now Peggy may bring food to the home of her ex and his wife, where she and the children gather for Thanksgiving dinner. She has learned to make the best of the situation, being comfortable with this new life story – not the one she would have written, but the one she is experiencing in real life. As the children have got older, they greatly appreciate their parents' efforts to maintain a friendly, co-operative relationship.

For discussion:
- Consider ways you may have put your young adult into an uncomfortable position.
- Discuss options to make arrangements with the children and your former spouse more amicable.

In the event of death

Renee remembers, 'I used to hate it when I would go to Florida for a visit and my mother would walk me around their condo, asking me what things I wanted when she died. It made me so uncomfortable, mainly because I wasn't ready to deal with the concept that she might die but also it was so awkward for me to ask for what I liked. However, after her death years later, I appreciated that she had made a list and everything was marked with my name or that of one of my brothers. It was easy for my dad to put together a package to send to us, knowing there would not be bitter arguments or recriminations. For the most part, we each got items that we preferred and that had special meaning.

'Shortly after my mother died, my father asked my husband and me if we would take care of him in New Jersey, should he become incapacitated at some future time. We assured him that we would be happy to do so. He also created a file for me with all the information needed as executor, plus a key to his home and one to his safe-deposit box. I cried through these conversations but when I got a call that he had died, I flew down to Florida, information and keys in hand, which made it so much easier to settle his affairs.'

While we don't plan to die any time soon and our children get equally uncomfortable when we bring up the subject, we have given each one information in the event of our death, including the name, address and phone number of our lawyer, accountant, insurance agent, bank accounts, insurance policy numbers and investment accounts. They know where to find the files for detailed information. We have advised them that we would wish to be organ donors and would not wish to be resuscitated if there is no hope of a normal active life. I haven't started taping their names to the bottom of grandma's silver tea service or Aunt Helen's crystal vase, but as I get older it might not be such a bad idea. We have seen siblings stop speaking for years following the dismantling of the parental home, even in the most modest of families where there was nothing of real monetary value, just memories and connections and history.

One man shared his experience with 'Dear Abby': 'I have read with interest the letters you have printed from readers about the difficulties they encountered when trying to settle the family estate after the parents pass on. Before mom and dad died, they let it be known that they didn't want any arguments or hard feelings during or after we kids divided up their worldly possessions. As executor of the estate, I felt responsible and had not yet devised a method for dividing the estate.

'The day we six brothers and sisters arrived at the homestead, mom and dad must have been watching over us. During the preliminary discussion, one of my sisters suggested that we put our names in a bowl for anything we wanted in the house and simply draw for it with no limitations. The next two days we spent together turned out to be the most heart-warming, enjoyable experience for all of us. I still remember my sisters ordering me to put my name in the bowl for an antique dish that I wasn't interested in but they thought my wife might like.

'I still have the small aluminum bowl with all our names engraved on it. I also still have the note my wife gave me as I left our house for the meeting: "Dear Bill, please remember that there is no material thing on this earth more important than family."'

Picking the executor when formulating our wills is another decision to be discussed ahead of time with our young adults. We may want to pick the son or daughter who is the most fastidious, or who has the most time. It is not an easy job, involving a lot of paperwork, phone calls, and tracking down of information. We need to approach our child with our thoughts and be open to their response. It is also important to decide on the amount of remuneration for the executor. An accountant or lawyer can best advise the amount, either via standard formula or depending on the complexity of the estate itself.

One other issue to raise for consideration was touched on in the chapter on financial issues. Allen had initially decided to leave his share of the marital estate to his sons, not to his stepchildren. This caused a major storm in family relationships and he later amended his will to leave some part to his stepchildren, though not as much as to his biological children. Other parents wondered whether to divide their assets equally or to give more according to need. The Gerbers have three children. Two are lawyers earning big salaries and one is a teacher who lives modestly. When preparing their wills they decided to leave more to the teacher than the other two children because he earns so much less. Still, they had concerns that it might cause problems in the relationships between the siblings once they were gone. Friends pointed out that circumstances might change, since no one can read the future. The lawyer might hate his work and become a teacher. The teacher might feel burned out and become a consultant in business. Another might become disabled. We owe it to our children to think carefully about the plans we make in the event of our deaths. Our purpose while living is to protect and nurture our relationships with them. We don't want to make plans that would create divisions, hostilities and irreparable hurt when we are no longer here to rectify the situation.

For discussion:

- Think about what provisions you have already made or need to arrange in the event of your death.
- If you haven't already done so, set aside a time to discuss these issues with your young adult. If you have not talked about these issues in a while, a conversation or a note to update children of any changes or just to remind them where important papers are kept is in order.

❤ In this chapter we addressed a wide range of topics that had some connection to legal issues. While not all families will be touched by trouble with the law, or divorce, we can be sensitive to those times when our children are having difficulties. We all need to prepare a will and leave some order to our affairs because no one knows the future. Money can become a gift or a curse, and there are no easy answers, no guarantees. It is an area that deserves much thought and open, frank discussion so that whatever plan is chosen, it has been carefully considered and all parties involved have shared their opinions and been advised of the plan.

Chapter 8
When relationships don't work

We have talked about many ways to encourage a positive relationship: communication skills; empowerment; being a supportive consultant, not an authoritative boss; being non-judgmental; having faith in our adult child's ability to find their own path; giving financial support when viable and/or appropriate; and opening our home to our older offspring. However, some parents experience a disconnection in their relationship with their adult child in spite of making every effort to nurture a strong bond.

Angie and Frank came for counseling because their youngest daughter had written them off. They were devastated. Angie had developed an ulcer and was having difficulty sleeping at night. She looked thin and frail, while Frank handled his hurt by focusing on his anger. As the history evolved, I learned that Daniela, or Dani as her family called her, was the youngest of four children. She was described as an easygoing, happy child who lit up a room when she entered. Angie had always felt particularly close to Dani as she was growing up. The trouble began, according to the parents, after Dani married Anthony and the couple moved to Texas where Anthony was offered a job working for his uncle. Angie and Frank noticed that Dani seemed upset with them when they would call, finding fault with something they said or did. After their first few visits to Texas, which they thought went well, they would receive a note or call from Dani complaining that Anthony felt slighted by them.

The relationship seemed increasingly strained. At some point, Dani got in a fight with her siblings about plans for her mother's 50th birthday so she broke off contact with them. When Dani called and asked her parents for financial help as they needed a new roof, Frank said he could give her $5,000. Dani angrily replied that wasn't nearly enough and hung up the phone. They later learned that Anthony's uncle gave them the $15,000 they needed. Angie cried as she related the next incident, which proved to be the final straw. She and Frank went to visit Dani and her family. There was some tension but overall Angie and Frank were enjoying the grandchildren and thought things were going well enough. Then Anthony started questioning Frank about *his* finances and how much money he made. Frank didn't feel he wanted to share his financial affairs with his son-in-law so he hedged the questions. Anthony got furious, said some nasty things to Frank and stormed out of the room. Angie showed me a letter from Dani saying that until they apologized to Anthony, her parents were no longer a part of their lives. Angie and Frank came for a number of sessions because of their heartbreak and frustration. While Frank didn't feel he did anything wrong, he was willing to apologize to Anthony, writing him a note saying he regretted any hurt feelings he unwittingly caused. They wrote letters, they tried to talk to Dani, to no avail.

Dani made it clear that Anthony felt her parents didn't like him and she was sticking by her husband. She pointedly explained that his uncle loaned them money, paid for them to travel to Paris, and was open about *his* finances. Interestingly, Anthony had no relationship with his mother or his siblings, finding fault with each one. Angie and Frank don't understand how their good-natured, loving daughter turned into this angry person who seems to question their love and intentions. They are particularly saddened to think they might not have a relationship with their grandchildren.

Through counseling, Angie and Frank were helped to accept that they have no control over this relationship. Every attempt they made to patch things up was rebuffed. It seems that Anthony has turned Dani against her own family and she is allowing it. Angie and Frank were encouraged to focus on the other children and grandchildren who live nearby, to find ways to enjoy their life as it is. After a year, Angie reports that she is healthier and sleeping better. She and Frank just got back from a wonderful vacation and her son and daughter-in-law just presented them with another grandchild. Even as she is feeling more positive about her life, she is aware of an ache in her heart that won't go away.

Larry and Lana feel they too have lost a child. Jack is an only child who had a close relationship with his parents. He married in his early 20s and was devastated when his wife left him after three years, saying she had fallen in love with another man. As he recovered from this loss, his parents were his strongest source of support. They kept reminding him he is a wonderful, kind, interesting and fun person and encouraged him to enjoy his life, not try to rush into another relationship. However, he found the bachelor life very lonely. After eight years of being single and having a few brief relationships that didn't work out, he met Erica.

Erica was a divorced woman raising two boys aged 10 and 12. They seemed to like Jack and he related easily to them. He started seeing more and more of Erica, 'helping her out' by fixing things in her house, lending her money, watching the boys when she had to work late. When he first introduced Erica and the boys to his parents, it went smoothly enough. Larry and Lana felt Erica had some rough edges and they were concerned about Jack stepping into a ready-made family, but when he announced their engagement, they determined to welcome Erica and the boys into the family.

Shortly after the wedding, Lana began to get calls at work from Erica who sounded inebriated. She would perseverate on some detail of something Lana did or said, trying to pick a fight with her. Lana debated whether to mention these calls to her son but decided to keep quiet, not wanting to interfere in a new marriage. Jack stopped in one day to tell them Erica was fired and they had had a huge fight. He slept on their couch for the night, then went back to work things out with Erica. Once Erica was home full-time, her drinking got worse. She refused to look for another job so Jack was now supporting four people on his salary alone. Erica seemed drunk and argumentative at all hours of the day. She began calling Lana and Larry more frequently, badgering them for their 'disapproval' or some similar complaint. The parents tried to talk with Jack about their concerns, suggesting that Erica needed some form of counseling. Jack would promise to talk with Erica but nothing changed.

After a year, Erica's rages began to affect her children as well as her relationships with Jack and his parents. She forbade him to talk to his parents. Weeks would go by and they wouldn't hear from him. Occasionally they would call Jack at work or he would stop in for a quick visit, saying nervously he had to get back home or Erica would find out where he was. Larry and Lana went through months of blaming themselves, wondering what they did or what they could have said differently that might have prevented this estrangement. They also keep wondering why Jack, this kind, gentle, attractive man who has so much to offer, would stay with this troubled, dysfunctional alcoholic. Jack has now been married five years. He keeps in touch in a secretive way. Larry and Lana have learned to keep the conversation light, letting him know how much they love him and enjoy hearing from him. They avoid any comments that might put Jack in the middle or make him feel guilty. They can't change Erica or make Jack leave her. They can only keep the lines of communication open, live their lives, and hope that one day they can have a full relationship with Jack and whomever is in his life.

Barbara's experience of loss results from a choice her parents made. When she became seriously involved with Tom who is a Catholic, her Jewish parents expressed their strong disapproval. When Tom and Barbara became engaged, her parents said they wanted nothing to do with the couple. Barbara has attempted to reach out to them, to emphasize her happiness with Tom, to no avail. Her parents have locked themselves into a corner.

We could go on with more examples of relationships that don't work. There are stories of parents becoming hurt or angry by a young adult's behavior and breaking off contact. A young adult who gets constantly belittled and criticized by parents decides one day she no longer wants to subject herself to this toxic relationship and pulls away. When a relationship between parents and an adult child seems to be at an impasse, everyone loses in a sense. Professional counseling may help the family come to some kind of reconciliation based on love and understanding, not on proving someone right or wrong. Some families are able to agree to disagree or have different perceptions and still maintain contact. They can place the emphasis on supporting a relationship, maintaining family ties rather than digging in their heels and holding onto their hurts.

Sad as it may be, when the relationship doesn't work, the child or parent needs to shift focus away from this hurtful part of the picture and onto the bigger picture of their life. Learning to accept what we can't control or change is a continuing challenge for each of us in some part of our lives. Being in charge only of ourselves means we can choose to expand our focus, choose to find joy, humor, playfulness and blessings in our lives. And, of course, there is always the possibility that the door that now seems closed may one day open again. But don't hold your breath or put life on hold or you will miss too many beautiful moments.

Chapter 9
Parent-shifting: opportunities for growth

As our children mature and develop their own lives, we begin to prepare mentally for the time they are no longer at home. It is a time of mixed blessings for most of us. We tell ourselves that we can't wait until they go off to college or move to an apartment so we can be unfettered and do what we want, yet at the same time there is an anticipated sadness for the loss of a part of our life. Yin and Yang – much as our son or daughter probably feels excitement for the new and sadness at leaving the known behind.

Feelings of loss and sadness – Renee's view

When you have been a parent for a majority of your adult life, the role becomes your identity to a large degree. Your children are the focus around which plans are made. We prepare meals according to their preferences and timetable. Weekend social plans revolve around their schedule – when they need lifts, have a sports game, or need us to be available in some way. I knew early on that I could get too dependent on my children's lives for fulfillment so I consciously developed a satisfying career in large part to cushion the blow when the children grew up. So I was caught off guard at the tears that spontaneously appeared periodically during our eldest child's senior year in high school. The thought of her not being around filled me with emotion. When Josh left next, I felt more prepared but it was still a loss in the contribution he made to family life. On the practical side, it was a shift to giving more time to the youngest now that Josh was no longer available to drive Sarah to activities.

Sarah was home alone for four years. At first it was strange to be three when we were used to being five, but she had a lot of friends and was very active with sports. I got used to having the phone ringing, kids in the house, cheering at her games. At the same time I took on extra responsibilities in the community and felt I had more time to devote to my work. I was looking ahead to the time when Sarah would leave and I could be even freer to 'do my thing' without feeling guilty that she was home alone, warming up leftovers for dinner. I was shocked at my reaction after taking her to college. I felt really sad and lonely for several months. Although I had always had a part-time psychotherapy practice, my main focus for 24 years had been mothering. Now that time was over. It took me a while to recoup, to get used to the quiet house and lack of activity. I missed the excitement of the field hockey season, coming home from work and hearing about Sarah's day. I missed the youthful energy in the house.

Then time went on and I found I didn't miss all the laundry or worrying at 1am on Saturday morning when she still wasn't home. I liked having time to myself. I shifted to a different way of planning and organizing my time. What eventually happened as I shifted comfortably into this new phase was a reverse reaction. It almost felt like a disruption or an invasion when one of our children came home for a visit. So this section is about some of the many shifts that occur and the variety of ways we respond at this time. There is an adage that says, 'Only two things in life are certain: death and taxes'. It is also inevitable that life is about change. We see our children grow, work through developmental stages, but we are ever evolving as well. Just as our body grows new cells every 60 days, we continue to have myriad possibilities for personal growth, especially at this time.

Men and women may deal with a sense of loss differently. Women may be more expressive about their feelings, talking about sadness, crying as I did even before Becky moved away. Men may have similar feelings but express them differently. Culturally they have been conditioned to be tough and, in their 'men are from Mars' way, try to fix it – or us. So a husband might tell his wife she was being silly or ridiculous, adding 'You can call her any time you want. She's only a few hours away. What's the big deal?' This same man might comment months later, 'You know, it's not the same around here without our daughter. I really miss her.' Everyone experiences many feelings, including some sense of loss. Your own feelings are not silly or immature or bad. You have a right to your feelings and don't let anybody make you feel embarrassed for those feelings. Respect yourself and your emotional life, it is just part of who you are. We can also be sensitive to the fact that others experience life in their own individual ways.

When you can be honest with yourself about your feelings, owning them in a non-judgmental way, you can plan more effectively. Bonnie knew she would have a very hard time when all her children were out of the house. Although she had held firm to a 'no pets' policy for their entire childhood, when her youngest entered high school she got a dog. Ostensibly it was for her son so he wouldn't be lonely at home without the other siblings. But anyone visiting her home and watching Bonnie with this puppy could see the obvious – this was her insurance card, her new baby in preparation for the anticipated loss in four years.

Freedom to explore new interests and dimensions

Many people dread getting older, feeling life gets boring and we start to physically fall apart. They see the wrinkles instead of the excitement. We suggest this can be a wonderful time – if we make it happen. Ann didn't think it was wonderful. She had had a terrible relationship with her own mother, whom she described as very critical and self-centered. She made it her goal in life to be a wonderful mom, as different from her own mother as she could possibly be. So invested was she in her children that when the youngest went off to college, she didn't know what to do with herself. She had a part-time job that wasn't fulfilling and her marriage was less than vibrant. Other than going to their kids' activities, she and her husband rarely went out. Peter was content to sit at home every evening and watch television. Ann wanted to go out, do something, but she said sadly, 'I don't know who I am anymore. I don't even know what I would like to do.'

Ann found it difficult to fill her time. She will have to make some effort to get back in touch with her core self. What makes her smile, what catches her interest? What part of her has been dormant, put aside, waiting for the day when...? She will have to find some answers or she may stay stuck in her routine.

Lauren, on the other hand, found so many ways to fill her time that she felt guilty. When her children moved out, her plan had been to get a job, doing something she didn't know. She had been a homemaker and a mother for 25 years so she had no specific job skills. Since there was no financial pressure to get employment, Lauren decided to take some courses as a way of exploring her interests and abilities. She found that she loved her Italian and gardening classes. Italian was hard but it was good for her ego to find her brain could study and learn something new. She found ideas in her gardening classes and decided to redo their backyard. She also joined a volunteer organization and spent several hours each week recording books on tape for the blind. Her husband commented that she seemed more relaxed, happier and easier to live with than she had been since they first met. Lauren is working to shed her self-imposed guilt that she isn't working and instead to appreciate this time of opportunity.

Nancy wanted to go back to college when her children got older and didn't need her home as much. In her 40s she finished her doctorate in psychology and at 50 started her own private practice. She is excited about the work she's doing and has built up her schedule to a busy full-time practice. Her husband, Frank, had been in the corporate world for 25 years. He hated it and couldn't wait to save enough in a retirement fund and savings to get out. As Nancy is discovering the pleasure of full-time work, he has retired and become Mr Homemaker. Frank does the cooking and baking. He loves to make elaborate desserts, then invite some friends over for coffee and conversation. Nancy isn't quite sure exactly what Frank does all day except that the house is clean, the errands are done and dinner is waiting. He follows the stock market and finally has time to indulge his passion for reading histories and biographies. Frank is delighted to be out of the rat race and just putter; Nancy is thrilled to be developing her professional life.

One more scenario suggests some of the many options open at this stage. Catherine was a widow with limited income and no marketable job skills. When her daughter, Edna, started to have children but needed to work, Catherine offered to babysit. Eventually Edna and her husband bought a mother/daughter home, where Edna's mom could be nearby and have some independence. Catherine comes over to her daughter's side to watch the children and returns to her apartment on the other side of the house when her daughter or son-in-law arrives home from work. Sometimes they invite her to stay for dinner, sometimes she cooks for them, but they respect one another's need for some privacy and separateness. Catherine is involved in her church activities, plays bingo on Thursday nights and keeps in touch with a few friends. It has been a great joy to her to be around young children again and a comfort to her daughter to have such reliable childcare.

All these paths are viable options if they are right for you – working, not working, developing a new career or interest, or being involved with grandchildren. The best approach is to use this stage to first decide what it is you would enjoy doing, then find ways to make it happen. Without children around, there's less housework and more free time. If I don't feel like cooking, we may eat out or just open a can of soup. It is easier to be spontaneous, to just get up and go somewhere, since there are no children needing attention, waiting for us, or restricting our schedule. And many find some relief seeing their children as young adults, knowing they grew up in spite of and because of us and for the most part turned out fine. (Don't forget, they are never a finished product to be introduced to the world at 18; they are still growing and evolving.)

As we may be wondering where our interests lie, we may also be feeling more secure in our friendships. Many women when newly married go to great efforts preparing for company. When we had friends over for dinner, I felt compelled to dazzle with the beautifully set table, four-course gourmet meal and at least three homemade desserts. Now I am comfortable inviting friends at the spur of the moment, making a pasta dish, salad and a dessert from the supermarket. I feel comfortable enough with established friends that I no longer have to impress or prove myself.

We also find ourselves losing some friends for a variety of reasons. One couple retires early and moves to California, another divorces and avoids socializing. We drift apart when our interests change. Or perhaps without our children as a bond, there is less to talk about together. While friends who have known one another for 20 years or more have a strong relationship in that shared history, it can also be a rich experience to develop new friendships at this time. The new friends didn't watch our kids grow up but, then again, they didn't see those anxious, neurotic years either. We meet on new territory, perhaps while on holiday or on a course we take. People meet us as we are now, and the relationship will develop because of common interests.

At some time in this phase we make the transition of accepting the ageing process. We notice less stamina and our memory fails us once in a while. We joke about having a 'senior moment'. The signs are all too obvious – new wrinkles, the gradually expanding waistline. While our bodies are ageing and changing, we don't need to feel old. Our grandparents at 50 looked and acted old. They fit the rocking chair image. Today, with our youth-oriented culture, we think of ourselves as young and act accordingly. We seem to be more health-conscious, more deliberate in our approach to eating and fitness. So we may be shifting, if we haven't already done so, to a lower-fat, lower-cholesterol diet as well as eating smaller quantities. Some of our new-found time may be used to play softball or tennis, join a yoga class, or work out at a gym. Weight-bearing exercises are particularly important for women as we age, to counter bone mass lost due to decreasing estrogen in our bodies. The fear of ageing need not govern our lives. Rather we can all become more Zen-like in learning to take each day as it comes – the precious present – and truly savor it.

As we age, our parents, if they are still alive, may begin to decline. For many of us it seems that when the children stop needing our care and attention, our parents are waiting to move into that space. When our caretaking responsibilities shift to an elderly parent, many emotional issues are invoked. No matter how old we are, it's never easy to see a parent becoming frail or infirm. Just as our young adults have difficulty accepting that concept when it applies to us, we want our parents to stay the same. There are other factors that make each situation unique but the constant is the sense of losing such a big part of our own history and realizing that our parents' deaths leave us as the older generation.

The amount of free time you have may be significantly impacted if you have an elderly parent living with you or nearby. The nature of the relationship largely depends on the history, whether you have positive feelings toward that parent and act out of genuine caring, or whether it feels like a heavy burden to watch over an in-law or a parent that you were never close to.

As with all the other shifts going on, it helps to be open and non-judgmental about our feelings and to be able to express these feelings to our partner, another relative or good friend who can really listen and empathize. Sometimes we excuse our children from this caretaking, wanting to protect them from sadness and rationalizing that they are busy with their own lives. Since this is part of the life cycle and we hope they will be compassionate people, it is important to include them when possible. We can ask them to visit grandma in the nursing home, stay for a weekend if grandad is living with us so we get a break. Maybe they can take half a day off work to drive a grandparent to the doctor instead of us being the only ones to do that. Our young adults may or may not be eager to help, but it is important that they help us sometimes, and important that they be asked to be compassionate toward others.

For single parents, refocusing on yourselves

Martha had been a single parent raising three children on her own for 15 years. Her former husband, an alcoholic, lived in another state and had little to do with the family. She had struggled without child support or help to work full-time and raise the family. When her youngest graduated from high school she felt it was now 'her time'. Although she would have preferred a partner, she found that she had become accustomed to making choices and decisions without consulting anyone. Martha had a few close friends, also single, and they began to spend more free time together. Instead of coming straight home from work every night to make dinner, do laundry, clean and keep an eye on the kids, she delighted in occasionally meeting a friend for dinner or going to a Tuesday night twilight movie when the prices were reduced. When home in the evenings, she reveled in actually watching a whole television program without interruptions or falling asleep. She had always been interested in crafts so she signed up for a class at the adult school in refinishing furniture and began to tackle some old bookcases.

Just the freedom to choose how to spend her time was a new experience for Martha and she loved it. For years all her energy and money had been taken up by the kids' needs. She thought she might feel guilty when she decided to go on a cruise with a friend instead of giving her son a down payment for his car. Instead she felt only a tweak of hesitation, then reminded herself that she had worked and sacrificed a lot for her children – now it was okay for them to work for whatever they wanted while she took care of her own needs.

Although Martha is an attractive woman, her children never thought of her as a date, only as Mom. As she started to socialize more and be out in the world, she met several single men and began to date. She had forgotten how good it felt to have someone open a door for you or pay the bill. After each date she would tell her children about the fun she was having. Much to her surprise, they weren't very happy for her. Her son got protective and worried that a man might want someone to take care of him or would think she had money. Her daughter couldn't say it directly but felt threatened that someone else might take up her mom's time and she would be less available for her needs. The 18-year-old son felt embarrassed to bring his friends over and find his mother, all dressed up, sitting next to a man on the sofa.

Not all grown children have trouble accepting – let alone encouraging – their parents to date. Some may encourage the idea of it but find they don't like the reality when it happens. Others become hypercritical of the person their mom or dad is seeing, partly out of concern for their parent, partly out of discomfort that the newcomer might not like them or fit into the family. One 18-year-old was very impatient with her mother, thinking she put too much emphasis on her relationships. Her mom would be in a great mood after she met someone. According to Sally, her mom would flutter around the house and agonize over what to wear and whether her boyfriend would call, more so than she ever did. If the relationship didn't work out, her mom became so depressed that she was miserable to live with for weeks until she met someone new. Sally thought her mother was acting very immaturely and placing much too much emphasis on having a man in her life.

If we are starting to date at this stage of our life, it can be a terrifying prospect. It is difficult to meet other singles, as there are few organized opportunities in our culture today. Once we meet, there are issues of grown children, jobs, money and physical intimacy to be resolved. Probably our young adults are not the most objective source of advice so a good friend, clergy person, or professional counselor may be helpful when we need to talk. Hopefully, the focus will be on adding fun, entertainment and companionship with friends of both sexes to enrich our lives, rather than that narrow goal of finding a mate.

For couples, redefining the marital relationship

We begin to catch glimpses of the future when our children are in high school. We are home alone on Saturday night and they are all out. One child goes on a scout camping trip and the other sleeps over at a friend's house. We actually have the house to ourselves for an afternoon and evening. During the child-rearing years it is not uncommon to find dad going in one direction, mom in the other, chauffeuring, doing errands, attending the children's sports games and activities. There is little time or energy to feel romantic. Once the children become young adults and are on their own, there is time and hopefully energy to focus on the marriage. For a parent who felt they came after kids and work, now is the opportunity to make the partner feel special. Without the distractions of children, you can have real, meaningful conversations. Go out to dinner. Bring home a takeout. Eat peanut butter and jelly sandwiches and watch TV together.

One study showed that married couples raising a family averaged a grand total of 19 minutes' conversation together a day. So it's understandable if you feel you don't have much to talk about since the fun and friendship part of the relationship has been undernourished. Start with finding one new activity to try together. It may be some form of exercise, learning ballroom dancing, computer graphics, or a cooking class. Or start the research for a project together, like re-tiling the bathroom floor. These activities form a bridge to strengthening the fun and friendship you experienced while dating.

When the marriage has a strong foundation, we can enjoy other aspects of this phase. One discovery is a sexual freedom that occurs. We can make love on Saturday afternoon and not be inhibited 'because the kids will know'. We can walk around naked, try different rooms, take our time. There is less concern about pregnancy so we can really relax, paying attention to our own needs and those of our partner.

Midlife crisis

Some couples struggle at this time. We hear the term 'midlife crisis' used frequently. One partner becomes unhappy with their life. They question their job, their marriage and their purpose for being on this planet. The origins of these feelings are often complicated and multilayered. They may feel they have worked so hard to be successful in their job but now discover they really don't like what they do. When you have a mortgage, bills and kids going off to college, it is hard to just walk away from a job and start a business or a new career. The partner may feel unimportant and neglected in the marriage, or be afraid of dying too young like their parents did. It could be a biochemical depression that seems to appear out of the blue or some other health-related issue.

People going through this vulnerable stage tend to look for a quick fix. Increasingly people are finding mystery, excitement and attention through chat rooms on the internet. One husband complained that his wife started staying up until two or three in the morning corresponding with her new friends on the internet. She was feeling unfulfilled and unappreciated. Eventually she told her husband she had met her soulmate. She left home and flew to another part of the country to meet this man. The reality was disappointing but when she returned home, she and her husband began to talk more directly and honestly than they had in years.

Neal had been irritable and distant for months. Every time Patty tried to get him to talk, he would snap at her to leave him alone. Finally they had a long talk lasting into the small hours of the morning. He listed all the stresses in his life, including his sadness when their son went away to college. He was upset about pressures at work, the loss of a mentor, but ultimately he confessed, 'I don't have any feelings for you. It's nothing you have done, it's just not there.' For 20 years they had been each other's best friends and she felt totally dependent on him emotionally and financially. When she realized the marriage might end, she initially panicked. She'd been home raising children for 18 years and had no idea what she could do. She found a job at a publishing company editing high school science texts, which utilized her college double major in English and biology. At first Patty had trouble adjusting to the full-day work schedule. She felt resentful that at her age, when she was anticipating more time together with her husband and an easier lifestyle, she had to go to work and was busier than ever. Gradually she came to realize the satisfaction of using her intelligence, getting positive feedback from peers, bringing home a salary. She felt challenged and valued.

While Patty found herself with a new routine, Neal had his own issues that he doggedly avoided for more than a year. He had always pushed himself to be the best. By the time he reached the top position in the company, he was emotionally and physically exhausted, though he didn't realize it. He found life at the top, with all its responsibilities, to be overwhelming. When the company lost money, he took it personally. He was devastated when he had to reduce the staff by 25%. Neal took the cutbacks as a personal failure. He couldn't get past the idea that his worth in life was totally dependent on producing, making a lot of money and being at the top – instead of just being. When he hit rock bottom – losing his job, his wife threatening to leave and his health suffering – his internist (specialist in internal diseases) suggested he attend meditation classes at the hospital's Mind/Body Clinic. While Neal thought this was a ridiculous suggestion, he signed up to appease his wife and doctor. The Buddhist monk Thich Nhat Hanh teaches a meditation to correspond to breath. 'When I breathe in, I calm myself. When I breathe out, I smile.' Neal learned, not without difficulty, to focus his thoughts on basic concepts of being. Paying attention to your breath. Being aware only of the present moment. Accepting the sacredness and beauty of all life as it is, including your own self. As Neal learned more about meditation and self-acceptance, he started to feel a sense of calm that was foreign to him. He noticed himself really listening to what others were saying to him, whereas in the past he would pretend to listen but his mind was on 10 other things. When he really tuned in, he noticed that he felt more connected. As Patty became more confident and independent, Neal was able to get more in touch with his emotional side. He felt more comfortable working on his own issues when he realized that his wife was not falling apart. Gradually, Neal and Patty were able to reconnect, finding their communication more personal and meaningful. Each became clearer about what they needed from one another emotionally.

Learning to live more fully in the present moment is not a cure-all but it is a beginning. As we teach or remind ourselves to simply notice and appreciate what is, we begin to let go of the anxiety and dis-ease that comes from over analyzing and judging past behavior as well as believing the future to be a possible catastrophe. Learning to stop judging ourselves removes the tensions of blame and guilt, and opens the door to a true sense of wellness and well-being. For those of us raised in a culture that promotes worry and negativity (if you are happy in the morning, you will be sad by night time), this Zen-like philosophy does not come easily but the potential benefits to our physical health and emotional well-being warrant some investigation.

Professional help may also be useful in offering support and guidance during this transitional stage. Some women, like Laurie, are afraid to go for counseling, afraid if they talk about their disappointment in the marriage that will mean the marriage cannot be maintained. Often it is the opposite. If you buy an older home or have lived in your home a number of years, there comes a time when many things start to wear out or fall apart. Taken as a whole, the job can seem overwhelming. Broken down with lists and prioritized, we can fix one or two parts at a time until the house looks vibrant and fresh.

For discussion:

- What changes are you experiencing in your life?
- Are you paying attention (being consciously aware) of your physical and emotional needs at this stage of your life?
- Share with yourself, your significant other or close friend what dreams you have for your future.

♥ Shifts during this stage of our adult years may come quickly or slowly but there are many: changes in our young adults and their lives (relationships, marriages, jobs, grandchildren); the ageing and passing of our parents and the older generation; moving to a different or smaller home; more or less financial security; changing relationships in our friendships; new interests; retirement; health concerns. What helps us get through it all is 1) attitude and 2) connectedness to others. In some ways, our children were the great distraction. Raising them kept us busier than we ever imagined. If life is a stage, it was full with people, activities and props. Now the children are still a part of our lives but more offstage. The props and people have been taken away and we are left alone, center stage, with the spotlight on one person. It is up to each of us to create the script, to bring our stories to new life.

Chapter 10
It never ends

So you thought the time would come when your job was finished? Your young adult has been launched into their independent life; now you can take off your parenting hat and shift to a lighter, less responsible hat – as if we can really separate off our parent role and put it on the shelf.

What we learn as we and our children grow older is it never ends. From the subtlest to the more direct ways, we remain connected to our grown children and would we really want it any other way? We experience the joy when our young adult marries, creates a home, finds their path. We have dinner together, go for a walk, or just hang out with these interesting people, seeing each other in a new light. It may be a time when they more fully appreciate us as parents and as people. The 'reward' for all that hard work comes at these magical times, as so beautifully expressed in a card from our youngest daughter, Sarah, when she was 24:

To my very first Valentines
Who taught me about the power of love
Who opened my eyes to the magic and wonders of the heart
And to passion
You have given me so much love
And it has made me so loving
I am ever so thankful for this love, and for you
My precious, lifelong Valentines.
Love always,
Sarah

For many of us, the happiness brought into our lives by grandchildren is indescribable. These fresh, wide-eyed innocents playing and discovering the delight in every little detail of life rejuvenates our own pleasure in a pebble, a butterfly, a storybook. Because of our accumulated years of experience, we are better prepared to parent without the anxieties and responsibilities that attended raising our own children. And we can hand them over when we start to tire or they get fussy.

While we share the joys in their lives, we continue in some way to share the problems and worries as well. No matter what their age, our adult offspring look to us for help in varying degrees. Our youngest has lived on her own for several years and is very independent in many ways. However, when she came down with a bad case of the flu and was feeling pretty miserable, her boyfriend tried to comfort her but she found herself thinking, 'I just want my mom.'

Becky and her husband were set to move into their first home. Then the closing date got changed. It got changed three more times at the last minute so that Becky was unable to find professional movers and they had to be out of their apartment. She called us to ask if we could help her move for the twelfth time. She apologized profusely, saying that she had promised after the last time that she wouldn't ask us again. But at crucial times, you turn to family first. Our young adults appreciate our help on everything from babysitting and loans to advice, which they seek but don't always follow.

One couple in their 70s abruptly cancelled their appointments and work schedule to fly to another part of the country after learning their daughter, aged 42, was being abused. Their daughter had not confided in them about the problems in the marriage. It seemed her husband was very easily angered and became verbally and physically abusive. She was terrified of him and his rages but hadn't told anyone. After her parents arrived, they helped her to look at her options and find a way to protect herself and her child. The Smiths found themselves caught up in their daughter's problems. For a long time their daily lives were colored by concern for their daughter's well-being.

There are the tangible things we do for our grown children and there are also the intangible things – the amount of mental energy and worry. The urge to help when there are problems, to protect from hurts and disappointments, to advise when their choices don't seem prudent in our opinion, to speculate on what might happen – all provide hours and hours of discussion over a lifetime. Our connectedness never ends.

In this book we have examined many of the issues that can potentially damage our relationship. Since every generation has its own personality marked by the economy, international issues and popular culture, we shift from a rigid and judgmental approach of what our young adult should do to understanding their social and psychological needs and working with their choices. As we have stressed, there are few rules or right/wrong ways to do things. Each family needs to decide its own beliefs and comfort level. But if our goal is to strengthen our bond with our child, we will continually strive to keep the communication open and direct, to be supportive and encouraging, and to work through conflicts.

We have explored the many shifts that take place both in the lives of our adult children and our own personal experience. There is one more shift that begins to take place. It starts in subtle ways.

Dale remembers, 'Several years ago I got very sick at a fundraising dinner. Renee took me to the emergency room of our local hospital. While I was being evaluated, she called our daughter who is a physician. At the time she was doing her residency and lived about an hour away. Becky got there as fast as she could and began to go over the chart, reading the lab reports and asking questions. She stayed all night and helped direct my care. It was the beginning of a shift to a time when our child can advise and/or care for us. Although in an emergency our young adult can be very solicitous, at other times they might balk at acknowledging our needs and limitations.'

When Becky and Bill first moved geographically closer after our granddaughter was born, Becky felt resentful when we weren't available to babysit more often. Although rationally she knew that we continue to have the same busy schedule we have had for years, emotionally she was disappointed that we weren't more available to her. These expectations and feelings of wanting more from parents can cause tremendous barriers in a relationship if they aren't talked about directly, acknowledged and aired without defensiveness and anger. Parents may feel angry that their child is never satisfied with what they offer. Young adults may feel angry as they still expect and want the infinitely giving parent rather than accepting us as whole people with full lives. There is a saying, 'Peace begins where expectations end.' For parents and children, a peaceful relationship is cultivated by a lot of effort, a lot of communicating.

As we noted in the introduction, there are thousands of books and articles devoted to raising children up to the age of 18. Resources to guide parents through the next phase of parenting are almost non-existent. The parents who shared their stories and concerns in our focus groups found the discussions extremely helpful. Often we hesitate to share problems concerning our young adult with friends or relatives, wanting to protect their image (and perhaps our own) and their privacy. So we end up feeling isolated or abnormal, as if our child were the only person to have that experience. Besides talking with our partner and child, it is very enlightening to talk with other parents of older children. Perhaps we can form parental discussion groups in our community to meet periodically and share concerns and questions. We have ample opportunities with friends and family to share the amusing anecdotes and happy news. But we need more support for those confusing and worrisome times.

After reading the original manuscript, our son Josh wrote us a letter with his invaluable comments that are included throughout the book. He wondered why young adults didn't list 'to be a good person' as a goal. Josh reminded us that our generation is responsible for shaping the world his generation is inheriting. As we continue to work to be emotionally supportive of our children, of ourselves and one another, perhaps we can extend our positive influence in a larger arena. Perhaps it is time for us all to work together to make a positive impact on the world community.

The actor Christopher Reeve, best known for his role as Superman, now experiences life as a quadriplegic following a spinal cord injury. At a college commencement address [university degree/high-school diploma ceremony], he advised students not to worry so much about instantly finding their life's work. He urged them instead to reach out, to give in their own way to touch the lives of others. He added, 'If you ever crash and burn as I did at 42 and experience regrets that you never did anything truly meaningful, you're going to have a hard time facing the future.'

The world is shifting so rapidly it's hard to keep up with the new technologies being developed every day. But people's basic needs don't change. While our life and those of our adult children change and evolve on some level, we continually work on sharing our love, respect and approval for one another, keeping our family ties healthy and strong. We move forward together, threads on a loom, creating new patterns. If we can be kind and positive, gentle and loving in the way we treat one another, we can move together in the 21st century making the world a little better, for ourselves, our family and for all its people.

The World Needs

A little more kindness and a little less creed,
A little more giving and a little less greed;
A little more smile and a little less frown,

A little less kicking a man when he's down;
A little more 'we' and a little less 'I',
A little more laugh and a little less cry;
A few more flowers on the pathway of life,
And fewer on graves at the end of the strife.

Author unknown

index